Countryside

Discover the best of rural Britain

Published by Time Out Guides Ltd, a wholly owned subsidiary of Time Out Group Ltd.
Time Out and the Time Out logo are trademarks of Time Out Group Ltd.

© **Time Out Group Ltd 2010**

10 9 8 7 6 5 4 3 2 1

This edition first published in Great Britain in 2010 by Ebury Publishing
A Random House Group Company
20 Vauxhall Bridge Road, London SW1V 2SA

Random House Australia Pty Limited 20 Alfred Street, Milsons Point, Sydney,
New South Wales 2061, Australia
Random House New Zealand Limited 18 Poland Road, Glenfield, Auckland 10,
New Zealand
Random House South Africa (Pty) Limited Isle of Houghton, Corner Boundary Road
& Carse O'Gowrie, Houghton 2198, South Africa

Random House UK Limited Reg. No. 954009

For further distribution details, see www.timeout.com

ISBN 978-1-84670-112-2

A CIP catalogue record for this book is available from the British Library

Printed and bound by Firmengruppe APPL, aprinta druck, Wemding, Germany

The Random House Group Limited supports the Forest Stewardship Council (FSC), the leading
international forest certification organisation. All our titles that are printed on Greenpeace-approved
FSC certified paper carry the FSC logo. Our paper procurement policy can be found at
www.rbooks.co.uk/environment.

Time Out Guides Limited
Universal House
251 Tottenham Court Road
London W1T 7AB
Tel + 44 (0)20 7813 3000
Fax + 44 (0)20 7813 6001
Email guides@timeout.com
www.timeout.com

EDITORIAL
Editor Hugh Graham
Listings Editors Alex Brown, Gemma Pritchard
Proofreader John Pym
Indexer Jackie Brind

Managing Director Peter Fiennes
Editorial Director Sarah Guy
Series Editor Cath Phillips
Business Manager Dan Allen
Editorial Manager Holly Pick
Assistant Management Accountant Ija Krasnikova

DESIGN
Art Director Scott Moore
Art Editor Pinelope Kourmouzoglou
Senior Designer Henry Elphick
Graphic Designers Kei Ishimaru, Nicola Wilson
Advertising Designer Jodi Sher

PICTURE DESK
Picture Editor Jael Marschner
Deputy Picture Editor Lynn Chambers
Picture Researcher Gemma Walters
Picture Desk Assistant Ben Rowe
Picture Librarian Christina Theisen

ADVERTISING
Commercial Director Mark Phillips

MARKETING
**Sales & Marketing Director, North America
& Latin America** Lisa Levinson
Senior Publishing Brand Manager Luthfa Begum
Art Director Anthony Huggins
Marketing Intern Alana Benton

PRODUCTION
Group Production Director Mark Lamond
Production Manager Brendan McKeown
Production Controller Damian Bennett

TIME OUT GROUP
Chairman Tony Elliott
Chief Executive Officer David King
Group Financial Director Paul Rakkar
Group General Manager/Director
Nichola Coulthard
Time Out Communications Ltd MD David Pepper
Time Out International Ltd MD Cathy Runciman
Time Out Magazine Ltd Publisher/MD Mark Elliott
Group IT Director Simon Chappell
Marketing & Circulation Director Catherine Demajo

The editor would like to thank David Anning, Berwick Car Hire, Chris Black, Cynthia Brouse, Alex Brown, Donald Campbell, Michael Graham, Nancy Graham, Sarah Guy, David Hirst, Lowri Jones, Cath Phillips, Mark Phillips, Tom Sunderland, Jill Turton, Eileen Whitfield and all the contributors to this book.

Maps Kei Ishimaru, Alex Brown.

Photography
Front cover Marshwood Vale at dawn, Dorset; Getty Images.
Back cover South Shropshire Hills, Edd Fury; Loch Etive, Dennis Hardley; Upper Teesdale, Michael Sayles.
Introduction Page 1 Heathland at Arne, Ian Badley; page 3 Affric Lodge, James A Gordon; page 6 Barrowburn Farm/Cheviot Hills, Don Brownlow; heather/Arne, Ian Badley; page 6/7 River Polly/Inverpolly, James A Gordon; page 7 buttercup/Ditchling Beacon, John Dominick; birch tree/Glen Affric, James A Gordon; snake's head fritillaries/ North Meadow, Adam Burton; Herefordshire cattle/Wye Valley, Harry Williams.

Pages 8, 10, 11, 12, 13, 14 Andrew Ray; pages 17, 18, 19, 20, 21, 22 Andrew Coulter; pages 24, 27, 28, 29, 31 Guy Edwardes; pages 33, 34, 35, 36, 39, 251 Ian Badley; pages 40, 42, 44/45, 46, 47 Tony Howell; pages 58, 61, 62, 65, 66, 67, 68/69, 253 Adam Burton; pages 88, 90, 91, 92, 93, 94, 95, 252, 255 John Dominick; pages 97, 98, 99, 101, 102, 104, 106, 107, 108, 109, 110 Leonard Smith; pages 113, 114, 115, 116/117, 118, 119, 120, 121, 122, 186, 188, 190/191, 192, 193, 195, 196, 197, 198 Harry Williams; pages 49, 50, 51, 52, 53, 54, 56, 57, 72, 75, 76, 77, 79, 81, 82, 83, 85, 87, 124, 126, 127, 128, 129, 130 Britta Jaschinski; pages 133, 134, 135, 136, 137, 138 Edd Fury; pages 140, 142, 143, 144, 146, 149, 150, 151, 152/153, 155, 254 Richard Wheeler; pages 156, 159, 160 Mike Pinches; pages 179, 180, 181, 182, 183, 184 Don Brownlow; pages 163, 166 (bottom right), 167, 168, 170, 172/173, 175 Michael Sayles; page 165 Photolibrary.com; page 166 (left) Natural England; page 166 (top right) David Hill/Natural England; page 189 (top right) RSPB; pages 200, 202, 203, 204, 205, 206, 207 John Wormald; pages 209, 210/211, 213, 214 Dennis Hardley; pages 216, 218, 219, 220/221, 222, 225, 226, 227, 229, 230, 232, 235, 236/237, 238, 241, 242, 244/245, 246, 250 James A Gordon.

Contents

Introduction

To experience sublime and romantic landscapes, British tourists once embarked on Grand Tours of Europe, where they were swept away by the majestic Alpine scenery of France, Italy and Switzerland. But in the late 18th century, their explorations were halted by the Napoleonic Wars, and Britons were forced to search for beauty in their own country. Inspired by the travelogues and paintings of artist and critic William Gilpin, who coined the term 'picturesque', travellers armed themselves with sketchbooks and watercolours and set out in search of wild places. With its dramatic and varied scenery, Gilpin's beloved Wye Valley soon became a substitute for the Continent; indeed, historians consider it the birthplace of British tourism. Before long, the Lake District and the Scottish Highlands came into vogue. For a period, the Grand Tour was replaced by the Home Tour.

Fast forward 200 years, and history is repeating itself. After years of far-flung adventures, many Britons are deciding to holiday at home, owing to economic and ecological concerns. And, once again, the rise of the 'staycation' has forced people to look at their country with fresh eyes, and find new destinations to replace the old clichés: the chocolate-box Cotswolds, mystical Stonehenge, cute New Forest ponies and the usual Lake District suspects. *Countryside* highlights what overseas visitors have long known: this small island has a huge number of possibilities.

To celebrate the renaissance of rural Britain, this book ventures off the tourist trail to discover pastures new, unearthing secret beauty spots, natural wonders and geographical curiosities. And there are plenty of geographical curiosities. Indeed, if you miss foreign travel, Britain has some corners that are downright exotic. There's a jungle at the Undercliff in Dorset (*see p24*), and subtropical plants flourish in the balmy microclimate of Cornwall's Helford River (*see p8*). Scotland's Loch Etive, a sea loch, has been likened to a Norwegian fjord (*see p208*). Spring blossoms worthy of Kyoto bloom in the Vale of Evesham (*see p124*), and botanists say the verdant Dinas bird sanctuary in

Wales resembles a South American-style cloud forest (*see p186*). The Roaches, in Staffordshire, are outlandish rock formations that call to mind the Wild West (*see p140*), while the South Shropshire Hills have been nicknamed Little Switzerland (*see p132*). And if you can't afford to be a space tourist, the barren and beautiful Inverpolly (*see p240*) in Scotland could be another planet. So much for the traditional green and pleasant views.

That said, *Countryside* doesn't ignore the classic destinations – it just zooms in on their quieter charms. In the Lake District, for instance, we steer clear of touristy Windermere in favour of the wild grandeur of Ullswater (*see p170*). Instead of the Yorkshire Dales, we zip over the border into the lesser-known but equally magnificent Durham Dales, for a glimpse of their waterfalls and wild flower meadows (*see Upper Teesdale, p162*). Most visitors to Wiltshire make a beeline for Stonehenge, but the Savernake Forest is just as awe-inspiring, with its mighty 1,000-year-old oak trees (*see p64*). No book about the countryside would be complete without the Cotswolds, but instead of the usual pilgrimage to the likes of Stow on the Wold, we make a detour to the less-trumpeted Owlpen Valley, a sleepy, fairy-tale idyll (*see p48*). And we even revisit the ravishing Wye Valley (*see p112*), which may have been popular in the 18th century but has lately been forgotten.

Natural assets take precedence here over the usual castles, cathedrals, stately homes and gardens. So instead of Sissinghurst, you'll find blankets of wild daffodils at Farndale (*see p156*) and a sea of snake fritillaries at North Meadow (*see p58*). In addition to covering new ground, *Countryside* challenges another rural stereotype: the Basil Fawlty school of hospitality. We have cherry-picked the best of a new breed of hotels, gastropubs and restaurants that emphasise service and style.

So why travel to the end of the world when you can just go back to the land? The countryside is waiting to be discovered all over again – let the new Grand Tour begin.

Hugh Graham

Helford River

Up the creeks – and into the woods.

Often when you visit the setting of a much-loved novel, you find the landscape has been disappointingly overpainted, or blemished by a pebbledash bungalow or a new hotel. By contrast, Daphne du Maurier fans will find plenty to feed their imagination in and around Frenchman's Creek – the small, unspoiled tributary of the Helford River that gave its name to her 1942 tale of passion and piracy. The love story between her heroine and a French pirate is played out along the river's hidden waterways and in the thickset woodland that grips the shores, and each page positively drips with romance.

With its 27 miles of spidery creeks, twisting channels, impenetrable woodland and tiny beaches overhung with oaks, it's easy to imagine the Helford River once provided a bounty of hiding places for smugglers, pirates and fugitives – rife in Cornwall, and particularly in this south-western corner, up until the 19th century. These days, the Helford River still attracts fugitives, albeit of the modern, law-abiding kind. They are attracted by the seclusion and timelessness of the place: here, roads allow just one vehicle at a time, life is lived by the rhythm of the tides and boating is the favoured mode of transport.

From the choppy waters of the open sea at the mouth of the river, to the small port of Gweek at its head, the scale gradually diminishes. The creeks, coves and inlets become calmer and more hidden, and the shingly beaches resemble perfect miniatures, looking almost like scale models.

In contrast to the raw impact of the north Cornish coast – with its dramatic moors, cliffs and stirring sea – Helford reveals itself slowly and seductively, with an unexpected glimpse of water through a thick tangle of trees, a pint in a thatched pub or the discovery that the ebbing tide has created a beach made for two – just in time for your packed lunch.

The scale and serenity of the landscape allow you to glimpse the intricacies of nature up close. At low tide, the sticky mud flats that emerge from the drained creeks are a fertile feeding ground for birds. Even without binoculars round your neck, it's easy to spot the white-bodied and black-legged egrets around the creeks, as well as grey herons, swans, cormorants and oyster-catchers. The seagulls that wheel endlessly overhead are also a constant presence here.

The shallow, sheltered waters of Helford are similarly abundant in fish, and the river has been designated a protected nursery area for young bass (any catch under 37.5cm must be returned). On the water, you might spot a grey mullet jumping, or a shoal of mackerel brushing the surface. Rockpools, which are best nearest the river mouth (try Prisk Cove), but also evident as far inland as Helford Passage (on the north bank), are lively with sea-anemones, crabs, darting blennies and gobies, prawns and even some rare species of iridescent seaweed.

But the most haunting natural spectacle is the dense forest that the river trails along its shores – some of the last pockets of wild woodland in the country. The twisted and tangled treetops are the result of a centuries-long fight for space – at points the greenery is so impenetrable that rain can barely be felt overhead. Streams percolate prettily through the whispering woods, sponged up by the thick moss and ferns that grow lushly alongside. Footpaths help breach the thicket, taking you deep into woodlands and down to the shore, where muddy banks and tiny beaches are draped with branches, and water ripples quietly in the breeze.

Further inland, sinuous lanes lead to heart-meltingly charming villages and hamlets – Manaccan, St Anthony, Gweek, Mawgan on the south side, and Port Navas, Mawnan

The Helford Estuary meets the English Channel at Nare Point.

Smith and Constantine to the north – dotted with thatched white cottages, village shops, pubs and church steeples that evoke a mythical lost England.

Du Maurier talks about Helford as a 'symbol of escape', of a place paused in time. And the effect on today's visitors is remarkably similar. Helford is one of few places in Britain to which time has been so very gentle – mostly due to its profound geographical isolation, the lack of fast roads and the commitment of locals to preserving its peace and natural beauty. The thread-like roads are still impossibly narrow, amenities are scarce (one-pump petrol stations with limited opening hours, no supermarkets and certainly no tourist information) and messing about on the river is still the favoured pastime.

All things considered, it's no surprise that the rich and famous have for more than 100 years angled for a slice of this secluded world, Du Maurier's Helford of 'placid waters' and 'refuge'. In fact, some of Cornwall's most sought-after houses are perched on the banks of the river, most with uninterrupted creek views and their own quays, all with astronomical price tags.

Still, house envy aside, the affluence of the area shouldn't get in the way of expedition. Mere mortals are still free to explore at will – and often in blissful solitude – the area's extensive footpaths, which weave in and around the pointy inlets and out on to the headlands, or sip a pint of ale at the water's edge, or take a dinghy out on the seldomly troubled waters. And those pleasures, we are pleased to report, are priceless.

The shores of the Helford River, pictured here near Helford Point, are lined with lush, thick woodland.

Subtropical plants flourish in Trebah Gardens, thanks to the balmy microclimate.

OTHER BEAUTY SPOTS

Thanks to the Helford River's balmy microclimate, subtropical foliage tumbles down to the river at the National Trust gardens of Trebah and Glendurgan. Steep, south-facing combes, they drip with palms, ferns, bamboo and other exotic greenery.

The Lizard Peninsula, south of the Helford River, has a wealth of pretty coves (Coverack, Cadgwith, Porthoustock), but the jewel in its crown is the distinctive Kynance Cove on the east side. In the right light, its sea-green serpentine cliffs, crags and stacks, turquoise waters and sugary sands bring to mind Bermuda, *The Tempest* and treasure islands. The beach is only accessible via steep steps from the car park, but the scenery is rewarding. Be warned: if there is mild to moderate swell, and the tide is high, swimmers – particularly children – should beware. There is a small café here, but nothing else.

Blustery Lizard Point is vintage Cornwall: rugged cliffs, jagged rocks and turbulent blue seas, topped by an 18th-century lighthouse (now open to visitors). You can join the record books here, at least for a few minutes, by being Britain's most southerly person.

Gillan Creek is one of several snug inlets.

WHERE TO STAY & EAT

The Shipwright Arms (01326 231235), on the water in Helford Village, was once a smugglers' hangout. Now it is a good spot for a pint and fresh crab sandwiches or a ploughman's overlooking the creek. Across the water, the riverside deck at the Ferryboat Inn (01326 250625, www.wrightbros.eu.com) is heaving in summer. Recently overhauled by the Wright Brothers – leading UK oyster wholesalers, based out of London's Borough Market – this old pub now serves upmarket food. The interior is decked out with a posh seafood counter serving local oysters and champagne. It's a rather incongruously urbane set-up, but there is no doubting the quality and freshness of the produce.

For exceptional food – and cottage accommodation – visit Trelowarren (01326 221224, www.trelowarren.com), a privately owned, 1,000-year-old estate in Mawgan, with hundreds of acres of woodland and fields stretching down to the Helford River, and impeccable eco credentials. The self-catering cottages are quaint on the outside, modern inside, and Trelowarren's contemporary New Yard restaurant is reliably good, serving a seasonally-led modern menu featuring local fish and platters of Cornish cheeses.

The four-star Budock Vean (01326 250288, www.budockvean.co.uk), on the Falmouth side of Helford River, is the last word in countryside pomp and ceremony, with traditional decor, vast gardens, a manicured golf course and lavish afternoon teas.

For a light lunch or breakfast – or a stroll around the 40-acre farm – stop by the lovely Tregellast Barton Farm, home to Roskilly's ice-cream (www.roskillys.co.uk) and the Croust House (01326 281924), a country-style restaurant in an old milking parlour.

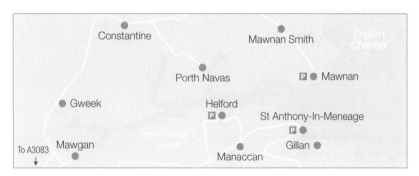

HOW TO GET THERE

The Helford River is in south-west Cornwall between Lizard Point and Falmouth. **By car** If you approach from the north or east of Cornwall, the Helford River is most accessible from Falmouth via Mawnan Smith. The closest dual carriageway is the A39. From the west, it is approached via Helston and the Lizard on the A394. The villages and creeks of Helford River are not well served by public transport. **By train** Redruth and Falmouth are the nearest stations (National Rail Enquiries, 08457 484950). **By bus** There are local buses daily to Helford Passage, the north side of the Helford River, from Helston and Falmouth (0845 600 1420, www. firstgroup.com); there are no buses to Helford on the south side, but a ferry makes the crossing (9.30am-5.30pm Apr-Jun, Sept, Oct; 9.30am-9.30pm July, Aug). **On foot** There are lots of footpaths around the Helford River. Our favourite walks are the short circular walk from Helford village to Frenchman's Creek, via lovely Penarvon Cove, and a longer excursion through Trelowarren estate's tall woods, in Mawgan, down to National Trust-managed Tremayne Quay, a tranquil spot only accessible by foot or water (ask at the Trelowarren reception for a leaflet with a map). **By boat** Helford River Boats (01326 250770, www.helford-river-boats.co.uk); Falmouth Pleasure Cruises (01326 212939, www.boattrips-falmouth. co.uk). **Map** Ordnance Survey Explorer 103, the Lizard; grid ref SW757260.

FURTHER REFERENCE

Falmouth Tourist Information Centre (01326 312300, www.visitcornwall. com). See also www.cornish light.co.uk, www.helfordriver.net, www.nationaltrust.org.uk, www.trebahgarden.co.uk.

Hay Tor & Hound Tor

Bleak beauty.

On a warm spring day, the grassy Hay Tor car park is the setting for a true cross-section of British attitudes to the countryside. Some of those emerging from their cars are geared up to the nines, expecting the worst of weather on the most arduous of moorland expeditions. Others spill out of their people-carriers in baggy jeans, T-shirts and stilettos, with tribes of dogs and kids, for a quick hoick up the hill. And yet others decant complete picnic sets from the boot of their car and methodically set up shop, right there in the car park, to soak up the moorland vibe and admire the view.

Hay Tor itself is an outcrop of granite that rises like a conning tower out of Dartmoor's eastern edge. After ascending from Bovey Tracey through Dartmoor's elegant foothills, past nestled manor houses and drystone walls, the raw, exposed tor hits you like a sock on the jaw.

This is the most visited of the moor's distinctive, 160-odd tors, gaunt granite outcrops in a variety of serrated, jagged and anthropomorphic forms. With a touch of imagination, or in dwindling daylight or sudden fog, these outcrops take on frightening shapes, and their presence adds to the forbidding reputation of the 368-square-mile wilderness of Dartmoor, the largest and wildest area of open country in southern England.

Climbers scale the summit
of Hay Tor (left); the view
from the top (right).

It's not a difficult climb up from the car park to the tor, a jumble of rock that has witnessed the fall of the dinosaurs, the Ice Age, and the arrival of the first humans 10,000 years ago. Today, it maintains its vigil like a fossilised mammoth, patiently letting the visitors clamber up its flanks using steps carved by the Victorians. On its brow, they admire the views down across Devon's verdant South Hams to passing ships on the English Channel, northwards to the distant dribble on the horizon that is Exmoor, and westwards across the moor's barren brown scab.

Most of this outlook is pastoral and innocent, but for many people, that barren view to the west is more than enough moorland for them, and they go no further than Hay Tor, fearful of the moor's legends and its changes of moods. Dartmoor is, after all, the location of one of Britain's most high-security jails (at Princetown), the setting for Conan Doyle's *The Hound of the Baskervilles* (specifically at the treacherous Foxtor Mire), and a place of regular search-and-rescue operations, as visitors often underestimate the moor. Myths, legends and (supposedly) escaped big cats stalk across its surface.

On a warm day, you certainly don't take your life in your hands by climbing up Hay Tor, but come in bad weather or in fog, and it is a different proposition, particularly if you're interested in history, and set off north into a world of heather and sphagnum moss.

It wasn't always a human desert up here. Back in the 19th century, there were as many as 100 men at work in the Hay Tor quarries, and in bad weather, it would be relatively easy to stumble and fall into their quarry workings if you weren't paying sufficient attention. For the 19th-century labourers, getting the stone off the moor was a huge physical challenge, so they devised a granite tramway that girdles the hill, to provide a firm surface for the wheels of their carts. The ridged ribs of the tramway are still very visible and form the basis for local paths.

There's more evidence of even earlier human habitation of this bit of moor if you keep going in a north-westerly direction, with the next tor – Hound Tor – as your ultimate destination. The distance between the two may be little more than a mile, but there's a good cross-section of Dartmoor landscapes en route, and fewer people at the other end. Even by walking 300 feet from Hay Tor, you'll quickly find yourself alone. Yet you may run into a couple of leathery Dartmoor fossickers hunting for so-called 'letterboxes' – plastic pillboxes that have been hidden in carefully recorded locations, and which are the target for an eccentric year-round treasure hunt peculiar to the moor.

Don't set off from Hay Tor without having your destination in sight, and make sure that destination is Hound Tor, and not one of the others. It isn't easy to tell all these siren tors apart, and each seems to beckon, saying 'I'm the one that you want'.

The route between the two tors descends through a jumble of loose rocks, and crosses a wooded stream, only marginally lower than the moor's tableland, but a lot more verdant, with glades, grassy banks and gliding pools. Up the other side, through banks of gorse and across heather that has been turned to charcoal by annual firings, you'll come to Hound Tor's medieval village, with its back to the moor, looking down into the easy life of forest and vale below. Even on a fine day, you can tell it must have been a tough existence trying to eke a living up here.

Hound Tor itself, supposedly named after a giant dog turned to stone by witches, has several clumps of rock in shapes that suggest an Indian chief, a bandaged mummy or a battleship, depending on your point of view. Being a bit further away from major routes, it is nothing like as popular as Hay Tor, and the local farmers use it as a meeting place during the hunting season. It is famous for its ghosts, has been used as a film set for *Doctor Who*, is the meeting point for the park's Halloween walks, and its legends may have inspired Conan Doyle. On a quiet evening, it could be just you here – and down in the layby below, the delightfully named mobile snack bar, the Hound of the Basket Meals.

OTHER BEAUTY SPOTS

Becka Falls, between Hay Tor and Manaton, is actually more of a series of dramatic tumbles than a waterfall, located on the picturesque Becka Brook. The owners of the land have created a theme park of sorts here. Christened Becky Falls Woodland Park, it charges an entrance fee for its animal shows and woodland trails.

Foxtor Mire, the model for Grimpen Mire in the *The Hound of the Baskervilles*, is a handful of miles southeast of Princetown. It is probably the only truly treacherous peat bog on the moor, and only hardy souls risk the walk around it (be sure to stay on the

Spooky Hound Tor is said to be a dog that was turned to stone by witches.

higher ground). The destination is the cross on the mire's south side, which marks Childe's tomb. According to the story, Childe was a hunter who got lost in a blizzard, slit open his horse's belly and climbed inside to keep warm. He didn't survive.

WHERE TO STAY & EAT

The Hound of the Basket Meals does fresh crab sandwiches and good fruit cake, and is in the car park at Hound Tor from April until October.

There's a charismatic thatched Dartmoor inn called the Ring of Bells (01647 440375, www.ringofbells.net) over in the pretty village of North Bovey, about four miles north of Hound Tor, serving quality British cuisine.

For accommodation, the Rock Inn (01364 661305, www.rock-inn.co.uk) at Haytor Vale, just down the hill from Hay Tor, is a sheltered, romantic spot that is popular with couples, who appreciate the cosiness after the bleak moor.

A good country-house alternative that is more central to the moor as a whole is the Prince Hall Hotel (01822 890403, www.princehall.co.uk) at Two Bridges, not far from Princetown. It has a wilder location, and is one of Devon's few dog-friendly establishments. The hotel places a big emphasis on the excellence of its traditional English dinners (roast guinea fowl, venison loin, pork belly), and rightly so.

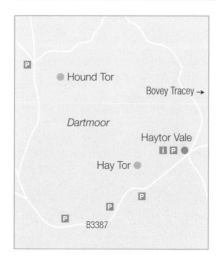

HOW TO GET THERE

Hay Tor is in Devon on the south-eastern edge of Dartmoor, south-west of Exeter. **By car** Take the B3387 west for four miles from Bovey Tracey, which is three miles west of the A38 Devon Expressway. There's a car park and visitor centre beneath the tor. **By train** The nearest rail station is Newton Abbot (National Rail Enquiries, 08457 484950). **By bus** The Haytor Hoppa bus service (01822 890414, www.dartmoor-npa. gov.uk), links Newton Abbot train station with Bovey Tracey and Hay Tor, and runs every Saturday from May until October. **On foot** Follow the path from Hay Tor car park to the top of Hay Tor. Hound Tor is about a mile north-west: you will descend into a small river valley and up the other side. **Map** Ordnance Survey Explorer OL28, Dartmoor; grid ref SX757770.

FURTHER REFERENCE

There's a visitor centre (01364 661520) beneath the tor, but the main High Moorland Dartmoor National Park Visitor Centre is at Princetown (01822 890414; for both, see www.dartmoor-npa.gov.uk).

Undercliff

Welcome to the jungle.

The air is sultry and the foliage lush. Tarzan could swing from all the hanging vines and tumbling creepers. In places, the vegetation is so thick, you wish you'd brought your machete and dressed like Indiana Jones. Birdsong echoes under the forest canopy, snakes slither among the seemingly tropical ferns and creepy crawlies lurk in the luxuriant grasses. Blur your vision and this could be the Amazon or the Congo; it's actually genteel Dorset. Yet the Undercliff – an eight-mile forest trail along the Jurassic Coast into Devon – has been dubbed Britain's only jungle, and it's not much of an exaggeration. This leafy tunnel combines Brazilian-style greenery, snow-white chalk cliffs and the odd tantalising glimpse of sea through cracks in the twisted branches.

A place for intrepid explorers, then. But the Undercliff is also for romantics. It was immortalised as a Victorian lover's lane in John Fowles' *The French Lieutenant's Woman*. In the novel, a scarlet woman lures a respectable gentleman to his downfall amid 'the inviting little paths' and 'shielding bracken and hawthorn coverts', features that typify this wild and overgrown English Garden of Eden.

Morals are not the only things that fall around here: cliffs do too. Described by Fowles as a land of 'deep chasms and strange bluffs', the Undercliff was created by landslides of the ancient cliffs above — an unstable mix of Jurassic, Triassic and Cretaceous rock. These crumble after being lashed by rain or destabilised by underground springs, leaving behind fossils on the beaches below, along with newly formed ravines that soon resemble what Fowles dubbed 'dewy green vaults'.

As the author explained it, all the landslips 'tilt [the soil], and its vegetation, towards the sun; and it is this fact, together with the water from the countless springs... that lends the area its botanical strangeness.' Hence the towering ashes and beeches, overgrown chasms 'choked with ivy and the liana of wild clematis', bracken that grows eight feet tall, and flowers that bloom a month early.

This fecundity is astonishing: it's as if the Kew Gardens hothouse exploded on the Dorset coast. In spring, the brilliant green is polka-dotted with colour: from anemones to orchids; honeysuckle to primroses; foxgloves to viper's bugloss. The grasses and herbs could stock an apothecary's shop: there's St John's Wort (nature's Prozac), Woundwort (once used as a styptic and sedative), madder (from the coffee family, a species of which is used to make quinine).

At one time, the Undercliff was even more exotic, as foreign plants flourished in the balmy microclimate, among them cherry laurels, holm oak, pampas grass, buddleja, wild arbutus and rhododendron. These plants have been purged by park rangers in a bid to protect native plants and the wildlife that relies on them, from the rare butterflies (marble white, wood white, painted ladies, silver-washed fritillaries) to the resident avian chorus (blackcaps, whitethroats, thrushes, marsh tits, blackbirds and bullfinches).

There are no parrots and macaws – yet (though, with global warming, they can't be far off). And, as befits every jungle, there are reptiles and creatures that make many shudder: grass snakes, adders, great-crested newts and blood-sucking insects (ticks). There is also a hint of danger (ticks can cause Lyme disease; guides recommend that you tuck in your trousers, cover your head and wear long sleeves).

Just as jungles hold an air of menace, so too does the Undercliff. 'To some it is wet, overhung, claustrophobic and frightening,' said Professor Denys Brunsden in the foreword to Donald Campbell's *Exploring the Undercliffs*. If you twist your ankle or come to grief on the tangled path, the only way out is by stretcher or helicopter, according to the wardens. Yet there are no mobile-phone signals to help you raise the alarm. Off the marked path, treacherous crevasses lurk in the undergrowth, waiting to trip you up. As Fowles put it: 'a man with a broken leg could shout all week and not be heard'. Which makes it a wonderful place to hide: two German POWs escaped from a local work camp in 1946 and hid here for months, drinking water from springs and raiding the larders of local farmhouses.

It's also a wonderful place to pretend. If you put on a panama hat and khaki trousers, you could be Rudyard Kipling. Those adders could be pythons, the brooks could contain piranha and Mowgli could be around the corner. Or you could be in a romance novel, and, as in the *The French Lieutenant's Woman*, stumble across a dashing gentleman or red-haired temptress in the undergrowth. That's the Undercliff in a nutshell – a place to let your imagination run wild, just like the landscape.

The lush and fecund Undercliff is dripping in ferns, foliage and curious plants and herbs.

OTHER BEAUTY SPOTS

Lyme Regis is a genteel seaside town brought to life by Jane Austen in *Persuasion* and later by John Fowles, who lived there. Today, it remains elegant and atmospheric, with its quaint back streets, pastel terraces and chalk cliffs. The beach is sprinkled with fossils (this is the western stretch of the Jurassic Coast). The Cobb, an ancient stone breakwater, is a local icon. Snaking elegantly into Lyme Bay, it hasn't changed much since Austen's day, still dotted with courting couples, weekend strollers and fishermen.

Bridport, east of Lyme Regis, is a handsome town with wide streets that host antiques stalls and farmers' markets. West Bay, Bridport's harbour, is a proper Dorset fishing village, known for seafood restaurants and a pretty shingle beach with sandstone cliffs.

Chesil Beach, further east, is the heart of the Jurassic Coast. The romantic shingle beach is sprinkled with fossils and inspired an Ian McEwan novel. It is also a refuge for swans, which live at the Abbotsbury Swannery, a moody and marshy nature reserve.

WHERE TO STAY & EAT

The Alexandra Hotel (01297 442010, www.hotelalexandra.co.uk), the local *grande dame*, is a Georgian mansion gussied up with boutique-hotel luxuries. The cliff-top gardens overlook Lyme Bay; the restaurant ticks all the boxes for posh, country-house dining. Next door, Hotel 1 Lyme (01297 442499, www.hotel1lyme.com) is a playful, stylish B&B that combines low prices, Designers Guild wallpaper and themed rooms, from swans to chinoiserie (one room even has a leather-belt motif).

The cosy Mariners Hotel (01297 442753, www.hotellymeregis.co.uk) has pink stucco walls, beamed ceilings and narrow passageways. It's all very Beatrix Potter (in fact, the author stayed here in 1904 and the building makes an appearance in *The Tale of Little Pig Robinson*). But there's nothing twee about the contemporary decor. The restaurant does quality pub food, roasts and local seafood; meals can be eaten in the garden.

On the waterfront, the Harbour Inn (01297 442299) is an elegant pub with an emphasis on fresh seafood. Hix Oyster & Fish House, a fashionably minimalist restaurant, is run by the celebrity chef Mark Hix (01297 446910, www.hixoysterandfishhouse.co.uk). The seafood (Lyme Bay fish soup, grilled Dorset blue lobster) is top notch, as is the sea view. There's no sea view at Jurassic Seafood Wine Bar (01297 444345, www.jurassic seafoodrestaurant.com), but the prices are down-to-earth, the fish is straight out of the water, and the kitsch decor – plastic sharks and dinosaurs – raises a smile.

For an atmospheric mix of rustic and right-on, the Town Mill Bakery (01297 444035, www.townmillbakery.com) has communal wooden tables, copies of Naomi Klein's *No Logo* and worthy, wholesome food: quiches, pizzas, salads and focaccias.

Foodies should try the River Cottage canteen in Axminster (01297 631862, www. rivercottage.net) for organic and local fare. In West Bay, the Riverside Restaurant (01308 422011, http://thefishrestaurant-westbay.co.uk) is a local seafood legend.

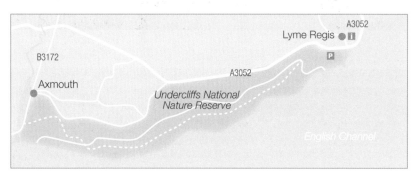

HOW TO GET THERE

The Undercliffs National Nature Reserve runs above the coast between Lyme Regis in Dorset and Axmouth in Devon. **By car** Take the M5, then the A358 to Axminster; A35 east for 1.5 miles, followed by the B3165 to Lyme Regis. Turn right on the A3052 (Pound Street) and then left into the car park past Cobb Road. **By train** Axminster station, then taxi 01297 34000 (£15) or bus (National Rail Enquiries, 08457 484950). **By bus** The No.31 from Axminster (0870 0106 022, www.firstgroup.com) goes through Lyme Regis. At the end of the Undercliff walk, buses X53 and X54 from Seaton return to Lyme Regis, but times are sporadic (phone First Group). Beer & Seaton taxis (01297 23366) will take you back for £15. **On foot** The Undercliff is a seven-mile path that takes four to five hours to walk. In the corner of the car park on Pound Street, follow the footpath across Ware Common until you reach the entrance to the Undercliff. Warning: do not stray from the main path as you could injure yourself in hidden fissures. To protect yourself from ticks, cover up and tuck your trousers into your socks. Sturdy walking shoes advised. **Map** Ordnance Survey Explorer 116, Lyme Regis & Bridport; grid ref SY345925.

FURTHER REFERENCE

Lyme Regis Tourist Office (01297 442138, www.lymeregis.org). Natural England (0845 600 3078, www.natural england.org.uk). See also www.jurassic coast.com and *Exploring the Undercliffs* by Donald Campbell.

Arne Heath

Splendour in the scrub.

On the edge of the Arne nature reserve in Dorset, at Shipstal Point, there is a lookout with a view of vast Poole Harbour. Below is a panorama of sea, sky, islands and beaches, with boats dotted like coral on a blue sea. To the east, lies Brownsea Island, where Robert Baden-Powell's Boy Scout movement set up its first camp in 1907, now a refuge of the red squirrel. Beyond lies Poole, and its renowned Sandbanks Peninsula, one of the most expensive pieces of real estate in Britain. On sunny days, pleasure-seekers scurry back and forth in their yachts and flashy speedboats, before returning to their luxurious, £10m homes.

Behind you, Arne Heath offers less materialistic pleasures. As the sounds of fluttering sails float up from the waters below, your mind turns towards the richness of nature. That's because the blue sea in front of you is backed by an ocean of green: Arne is where ancient heathland merges with marshland and saltwater. Instead of yachts, this interior sea is sprinkled with Scots pines amid gorse, heather and grasses; instead of the jet set, Arne's residents are feathered flyers (the land is owned by the RSPB).

Though very green, Arne is not lush. Much of it is rather sparse and scrubby, owing to the sandy, acidic soil that characterises dry heathland. But it is also a haunting place – around the world, heathlands are now more rare than tropical rainforests. Its majesty is subtle, its beauty an enigma: not quite the coast, yet not quite terra firma; spartan, but naturally rich; tough, but fragile. On a summer day, the land seems parched, yet there are soggy patches with reed beds and wading birds. Its curious effect tends to linger, and leave you wistfully plotting your return.

Arne is part of Dorset's Purbeck Heaths: dry, sandy lowlands that were established in Britain over 4,000 years ago. Perhaps the ancient provenance of heathland adds to its mystique. This is not a natural landscape, but one whose mosaic has been sculpted by centuries-old human intervention, ever since man started to fell trees for fuel and building materials or to clear land for livestock. What we imagine as 'wild' is, in fact, the product of man's urge to create architecture.

Still, these heaths have come to be valued by conservationists. In the past 200 years, Europe has lost 90 per cent of its heathland habitats; Dorset's heathland once covered 120,000 acres, but only 17,000 acres remain, owing to changes in farming, forestry plantations, urban expansion and road building. As a result, almost all Dorset heathland has been designated as a Site of Special Scientific Interest. And conservationists work hard to keep the pine trees in check, because heaths support more wildlife than wood-lands do. Arne's 1,000 acres provide shelter to 220 bird species, 31 mammal species and nearly 500 flowering plants, and swarms of insects: 850 species of moth, 33 butterfly species and 23 dragonfly species. And a herd of more than 400 Sika deer roam the reserve.

These numbers are impressive, but Arne is less a list-maker's paradise than a place for contemplation. You might, for instance, ponder just how the swift, which gathers here in flocks before dusk, can sleep in flight (it is the only bird known to do so), or how the raft spider, Britain's largest, manages to hurtle across the surface of Arne's acidic bogs.

The swift's airborne somnambulism is remarkable, but it is just one of thousands of birds that make Arne their habitat. Birds, indeed, were Arne's initial raison d'être: the RSPB first acquired land at Arne in 1965 to save the Dartford warbler. At the time, there were

Arne is a sea of purple in August when the heather blooms; Corfe Castle was the inspiration for Enid Blyton's Kirrin Castle.

only 11 pairs nationally, with two at Arne; now Arne alone has 55 pairs. The reserve has two hides, one on the lesser-visited Combe heath side, while the other overlooks the marshland of Arne Bay. Both showcase an avian revue: sandwich and common terns, black-tailed godwits, little egrets, avocets, oyster-catchers and hen and marsh harriers. Dark-bellied brent geese graze nearby fields; during the evening, the sound of owls hooting and and the strange churring trill of nightjars fill the air.

But the daylight shows off Arne at its best. On a summer morning, any of Britain's six native reptiles – the sand lizard, common lizard, smooth snake, adder, slow worm and grass snake – may be seen slithering in the sand. The purple heather and yellow gorse blaze in the sun, and the sight of the blue sea is a cool contrast to the baked landscape.

Arne is no less alluring during inclement weather. Rain, mist and snow lend a melancholy tinge to the ancient heathland. The ruins of Corfe Castle, visible to the west, enhance the forlorn feel. As visitors wander the tranquil trails once trodden by Neolithic man, they may hear echoes of ancestors past – along with the call of the birds and the song of the sea. And they will see an ancient, scrubby British landscape that stubbornly clings on in the face of modern encroachment. Suddenly the champagne and yachts of Sandbanks seem far away indeed.

OTHER BEAUTY SPOTS

Compared to the rest of Britain, Dorset is uncommonly blessed with heathland. Nearby Stoborough Heath and Hartland Moor are similar in feel to Arne, barren landscapes that brim with life. Typical heathland plant species include the rare bog orchid, marsh gentian and the dwarf and common gorse. Indigenous invertebrates include the rare wartbiter cricket and dragonflies of the golden ringed, ruddy darter and keeled skimmer variety. Local bird species are the nightjar, Dartford warbler, merlin and skylark.

Studland Beach, a ferry ride away from Sandbanks, has a touch of the Caribbean about it: on sunny days, the sands are sugary white, the water turquoise. The beach is three miles long, stretching from Shell Bay to the chalk cliffs of Handfast Point and Old Harry Rocks. Naturists bare all on Knoll Beach; families swim further south by the National Trust café. Behind the dunes is an otherworldly interior of sand, grasses, gorse and heather.

Corfe Castle, dating back to the 11th century, is visible from the Combe Heath hide at Arne. Commanding a gap in the Purbeck Hills between Wareham and the seaside town of Swanage, this romantic ruin is at once stunning, mysterious and bursting with history. It is also the source of literary and cinematic inspiration: the castles in Enid Blyton's adventure stories were based on Corfe, while the two main characters in Mike Leigh's film *Nuts in May*, Keith and Candice-Marie, visit the castle during their camping holiday.

Arne's natural assets are legion, from the herd of Sika deer to the great tits (bottom left) and cormorants and gulls (left).

WHERE TO STAY & EAT

The Dorset Heaths are not geographically remote – in fact, many of them co-exist with urban sprawl – but those of Arne, Stoborough and Hartland have an off-the-beaten-track feel by dint of Dorset's rambling 'A' and 'B' roads. B&Bs are thin on the ground, and many visitors opt to stay in nearby towns such as Wareham, Swanage and Poole.

The Haven Hotel (01202 707333, www.fjbhotels.co.uk) is an upmarket art deco property right on the sea in Sandbanks. It's so close to the water, in fact, that you could go to sleep listening to the sound of waves; indeed, most rooms have views of the sea, either towards Studland Beach or Brownsea Island in Poole Harbour.

For food, The King's Arms in Stoborough (01929 552705, www.thekingsarms-stoborough.co.uk) has a stellar reputation for traditional British cooking from locally sourced ingredients. With an inn on this site for 400 years – Oliver Cromwell's troops were billeted here during the siege of Corfe Castle in 1643 – it has a venerable history, too.

In Studland, the Bankes Arms Country Inn (01929 450225, www.bankesarms.com) is a quaint, ivy-covered stone hotel with a great beer garden; its bedrooms are cheap and not very cheerful, but the cosy pub does good, homely meals, including fresh seafood. The Shell Bay Seafood Restaurant and Bar (01929 450363, www.shellbay.net) has a bright and breezy setting on Poole Harbour, and a menu that emphasises freshly caught fish (Dorset crab, sea bass, lemon sole and sardines).

HOW TO GET THERE

Arne Heath lies on the west side of Poole Harbour in Dorset. **By road** The A35 is the nearest major road. Turn off the A35 on to the A351 heading south. Follow the signs for Wareham. From Wareham town centre, go south over the causeway to Stoborough. Arne is signposted from here, the car park is near the entrance to Arne village. To get to Arne from Sandbanks, take the 'Bramble Bush Bay' chain ferry to Shell Bay at Studland, which runs about every 20 minutes. Then take the B3351 to Corfe Castle and the A351 towards Stoborough.
By train Wareham, four miles from Arne, is the train station nearest to the reserve (National Rail Enquiries, 08457 484950).
By bus The nearest bus stop to Arne is at Stoborough, three miles from the reserve. From Bere Road in Wareham, take the Wilts & Dorset no.40 towards Swanage (0871 200 2233, www.wdbus.co.uk). **On foot** The Arne Reserve is three miles from Stoborough. The Shipstal and Coombes trails are open at all times, but the car park closes at dusk. Shipstal Point, overlooking Poole Harbour, is on the eastern edge of the reserve. **Map** Ordnance Survey Explorer OL15, Purbeck & South Dorset; grid ref SY975885.

FURTHER REFERENCE

Purbeck Information & Heritage Centre (Wareham, 01929 552740, www.visit swanageandpurbeck.com). Royal Society for the Protection of Birds (01929 553360, www.rspb.org.uk).

Arne overlooks
Poole Harbour.

Somerset Levels

Walk on water.

If global warming and the concomitant rise in the oceans turns out to be reality, then there'll be one part of the English countryside where the return of the sea will come as no surprise: the Somerset Levels. For it wasn't so long ago that this pancake-flat tract of land spent most of its year underwater.

Even today, the onset of winter in the Levels usually heralds an annual makeover that draws great bedsheets of the wet stuff up around villages of honey-coloured limestone. These seasonal sheets of water are stitched by marching rows of pollarded willow trees, which are decorated with coots, Bewick's swans and other migratory wetland birds, and threaded by raised dykes bearing walkers in wellies.

There are not many parts of the British countryside that look their best in the winter, but this is one of them. As the lowering skies flicker with bird life, the landscape seems to dissolve into the distance, seeping away in the mist, and the lonely cry of the curlew rolls across the marshland, as it has done for hundreds of years.

Winter is also the time of year when the locals park their vehicles on high ground and resort to tractors for the school run, and rabbits have been known to climb up on to the backs of sheep to stay dry. So if, and when, the sea level rises for good, the Levellers will have had plenty of dress rehearsals.

The Somerset Levels are essentially the peaty floodplains of the rivers Parrett, Huntspill, Brue and the King's Sedgemoor Drain. The whole area was once a semi-permanent inland sea that stretched all the way along the southern edge of the Mendip Hills to the Bristol Channel. Six thousand years ago, it was inhabited by eel hunters who lived in villages that were built on stilts, and travelled by boat or on tracks of woven hurdles laid on top of the marshes.

As water levels gradually subsided, so cattle herders began to move their animals on to the emerging, silt-enriched summer grasslands. This may have given rise to the name Summersaeta – 'the land of the summer people' – from which Somerset gets its name.

The Domesday Book records fisheries still here in the 11th century, and the region's remoteness attracted early monks in search of meditative isolation, who founded monasteries at Glastonbury, Muchelney and Athelney (the –ey ending means 'island', as in Guernsey, Jersey and Alderney). It was their more commercially minded successors who first took the water problem in hand in the 13th century, after they grew tired of being cut off every winter. They initiated the now complex drainage system, overlaying the marshland with straight lines and creating big belts of grassland.

Today, the mean elevation of the Levels is just 12 feet above current sea level, even as far as 30-40 miles inland, and plenty of areas are well below that. Meanwhile, the high tides in the Bristol Channel regularly reach 20 feet above sea level, which explains the continuing need for dykes and pumping stations.

The landscape is at its most mystically and mythically distinctive along the banks of the river Parrett near Langport. Raised banks, exuberant burdock and walls of whispering reeds give tantalising glimpses of cattle pastures that seem to stretch unbroken into the distance, but they also conceal somnolent eel-rich ditches, veins of water that flow in either direction, depending on time and tide. Sometimes the bigger waterways resemble ribbons of sky sliced from the clouds, and in the splendour of summer, smaller ditches acquire a layer of algae that blends them into the meadows, deceiving goose-chasing dogs, who charge in at full speed and emerge looking foolish.

Here, Muchelney Abbey may be in ruins, thanks to Henry VIII, but its setting is essentially as it was in medieval times – still isolated by winter floods on its own little

The Somerset Levels, as seen from Kingsbury Episcopi, are pancake-flat floodplains that were once under the sea; a willow crop by a rhyne near Stoke St Gregory (overleaf).

shallow rise, and yet to be absorbed by any incipient housing estate. Nearby Athelney, where King Alfred supposedly made a hash of his buns while hiding from the Danish army in 878, is today just a grassy mound, but in those days was surrounded by swampy marsh and only approachable by punt. Today, only Burrow Mump rises out of the winter water as it always has, still church-topped, a lung-bursting hill-climb that will be rewarded with dramatic views in all directions over a tessellated land. The church itself, like the abbeys, is a ruin, but it has an unmistakeable aura and anyone who climbs to the top won't be surprised to learn that the Mump is on a ley line that joins Cornwall's St Michael's Mount with Glastonbury, Avebury and Bury St Edmunds.

All of these charismatic locations are within walking distance of each other on the Parrett Trail, which runs along high dykes past rhynes, sluice gates and pumping stations. Walk this route in winter, and you'll see water management in action: some fields are used as overflow reservoirs, while the pumps work hard to get the run-off down to the sea.

The Parrett Trail runs all the way from the river's source to its estuary, a distance of 50 miles, along a waterway that was a major highway in the 18th and 19th centuries as the bargees took advantage of the huge tides to move in and out with loads of willow, wheat, gravel, reeds, potatoes, coal and fish.

Some of that trade has been recorded in the trail's stiles, seats and bridges, specially made by local artists. Indeed, the local bargees seem to have been replaced by creative types. They include John Leach, a jolly, shaggy figure who has been fashioning pots at Muchelney Pottery for 40 years. And Serena de la Hey at Stoke St Gregory, who bends the Levels' most traditional crop to her will, making geese, swans and running dogs out of willow. Her most famous creation is the Running Man, a huge willow giant alongside the M5 motorway just north of Bridgwater, welcoming visitors to the southwest.

The Levels is the only place in the UK where willow is still commercially farmed. The drastically pollarded trees make angry fists around Stoke St Gregory, where the Willows and Wetland Centre has demonstrations and displays on the various types and uses of willow in today's world. The 'withy' is still harvested by hand and variously stripped, steamed and boiled, depending on its end use.

Due south of Stoke St Gregory is a slice of the Levels where man has stepped back from all but the most traditional land management. West Sedgemoor is an RSPB reserve, and one of the richest sites for breeding waders in south-west England. One of England's largest remaining wet meadows, it spreads over 103 acres of woodland and 1,000 acres of hay meadow and wetland, and there's a particularly good vantage point from the Scarp Trail to look down over the old field structures that were first shaped by those busy monks. Step out of your car here on a warm spring day, and the sound effects will tell you it's a paradise for birds; but purists arrive in winter, when teal can be spotted among the flocks of wildfowl and waders, and the Levels' moody ambience comes into its own.

OTHER BEAUTY SPOTS

The most dramatic natural attraction in these parts is the Cheddar Gorge, up in the Mendips. The largest gorge in the United Kingdom, it is also the location of the Cheddar Caves, where Britain's oldest complete human skeleton, estimated to be 9,000 years old,

was found in 1903. Because of these headlines, the limestone gorge lures hordes of tourists, so visit in the early morning or in the evening.

To the east side of the Levels stands Ham Hill, above the village of Norton-sub-Hamdon. Ham is the site of an ancient Iron Age fort, and it dominates the area, not just for its size and the views it affords in all directions, but also because its quarries have provided the lovely, honey-coloured stone that characterises the local villages. Crowned with grassland and encircled with the ridges of old ramparts and earthworks, it has strange-shaped crags and outcrops, and is locally managed as a 400-acre country park.

WHERE TO STAY & EAT

Anyone walking the Parrett Trail should try to arrive at the village of Kingsbury Episcopi in time for lunch. Here the Wyndham Arms (01935 823239, www.wyndhamarms.com) has a log fire, pies, steak and sausage, and cider from the nearby Burrow Hill Cider Farm. The popular Half-Way House at Pitney (01458 252513, www.thehalfwayhouse.co.uk) is an unreconstructed flagstoned pub with huge pine tables, copies of *Private Eye* and the newspapers, real ales and – in the evenings – a choice of homemade curries.

In the mystical heart of the flatlands, the cosy and tasteful Muchelney Ham Farm (01458 250737, www.muchelneyhamfarm.co.uk) is a high-end B&B set in a 17th-century farmhouse. For something more formal, Farthings Country House Hotel in Hatch Beauchamp (01823 480664, www.farthingshotel.co.uk) is handsome and personally run.

The Willow Man is the most famous sculpture by local artist Serena de la Hey, who also fashions geese, swans and dogs from 'the withy'.

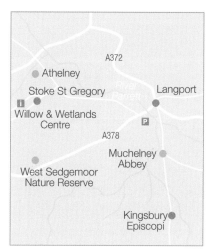

hiring out bicycles – it has a range of brochures and the Parrett Trail walkers' pack. **By train** Taunton and Yeovil are the nearest stations to Langport (National Rail Enquiries, 08457 484950). **By bus** The no.54 bus (01823 272033, www.firstgroup.com) goes from Yeovil and Taunton to Langport. **On foot** Pick up the Parrett Trail, a 50-mile path, at Langport for some classic Somerset Levels countryside (www.riverparrett-trail.org.uk). **Map** Ordnance Survey Explorer 129, Yeovil & Sherborne; grid ref ST420264.

HOW TO GET THERE

The Somerset Levels sit between Wells, Glastonbury and the sea. **By road** The Levels are accessible from the M5 junction 23. For a good jumping-off point, go to the River Parrett Visitor Centre in Langport. Although not an official tourist information centre – its main business is

FURTHER REFERENCE

River Parrett Visitor Centre (Langport, 01458 250350, www.southsomerset. gov.uk). RSPB at West Sedgemoor (01458 252805, www.rspb.org.uk/reserves). Willows and Wetland Centre (Stoke St Gregory, 01823 490249, www.englishwillowbaskets.co.uk).

Owlpen Valley

A sleeping beauty.

'Owlpen in Gloucestershire – ah! What a dream is there!' wrote a wistful Vita Sackville-West in 1941. Nearly 70 years on, her words remain true, for Owlpen is a place that seems to exist outside time. Its quaint Tudor manor house was once nicknamed 'Sleeping Beauty' after it lay dormant for 100 years, and the name is apt: this dreamy Cotswold valley could easily have been the setting for the fairy-tale about the slumbering princess. And its cosy romance would have impressed Arts and Crafts master William Morris, an early convert to the charms of the Cotswolds.

Tucked in the cleft of what the late (and local) poet UA Fanthorpe described as a 'narrow, hand-carved valley', Owlpen – a tiny parish with a house, church and cottages set amid woodland and meadow – is hidden from the world (and the Cotswold tourist hordes). It is also one of the deepest and steepest valleys along the Cotswold Escarpment – you don't so much stumble upon it, as into it.

Winding downwards through dense woods towards the promise of wild-flower meadows – 'meads' in the local parlance – the keen-eyed catch glimpses of a diminutive manor house, all soft buttery limestone framed by dark greenery. A local 18th-century historian, Samuel Rudder, called it 'a kind of gloomy retreat... The church and houses lie dispersedly at the top of a deep and narrow combe, almost environed by steep hills, covered with hanging beech woods, and forming a kind of amphitheatre.'

Perhaps Rudder was right. The scenery *is* a bit gothic: the shadowy ranks of beech loom almost ominously over the quiet valley. And there is a certain gloominess here on a rainy day, when the light is swallowed up by ancient thickets and the steep banks. But in the sunshine, it is glorious (Prince Charles once called it the epitome of the English countryside). Whatever the weather, Vita and the Prince were on to something: it is a magical place, suffused with a mysterious atmosphere, its history an audible hum.

The Saxons left a lasting legacy in the form of pleasingly evocative place names. Fiery Lane, a hedgerow-narrowed road, is actually a corruption of an ancient word meaning 'wooded hill'. In the same misleading vein, both Blacknest Lane and Peter's Nest Cottage do not derive their meaning from birds' nests, but from 'ness', a dark, wooded place. Likewise, the name Owlpen does not refer to the wisest of birds (though the roof of the manor sports two carved stone owl finials), but a village headman called Olla, who first settled here in the 9th century; 'pen' referring to the enclosure he established.

The winsome scenery lives up to the curious monikers. Many of the footpaths connect with the Cotswold Way – a bucolic trail that stretches 100 miles from Chipping

One of the deepest valleys in the Cotswolds, Owlpen feels both pastoral and gothic.

Campden to Bath. Some paths lie deep in the beech and elm woods, the sunlight dappling the ground where the canopy allows. Others lead you abruptly out into the open and a landscape fit for a Morris & Co design, all variegated green and gold patterns. At the top of the Ewelme Brook path, there's a Bronze Age round barrow; below a bewitching vista. From above, new details of the Manor House emerge: the tiered gardens, the trio of mismatched gables added over centuries (1450, 1540 and 1616).

In 1471, the chaos of the outside world briefly impinged on Owlpen. Queen Margaret of Anjou, wife of Henry VI, stayed at Owlpen en route to that great battle of the War of the Roses at Tewkesbury, where she lead the losing Lancastrian side. Her ghost, clad in a fur-trimmed gown, is said to walk the Great Chamber on the third night of every May, the anniversary of her visit.

When the last of the medieval de Olepenne family died in 1815, the new owners abandoned the manor for a time. The old manor slumbered on in the shelter of the valley, the yew trees eventually dwarfing it, while formidable boughs of ivy, as thick as a man's

thigh, enveloped its façade; for a century, it lay empty, hence the Sleeping Beauty comparisons. In 1925, the Arts and Crafts architect Norman Jewson bought the house for £3,200, and painstakingly revived it; 'repairing never restoring,' as he put it. The Mander family have lived here since 1974 and continue Jewson's work.

The manor's small garden is one of the earliest examples of an English formal garden and is both charming and spooky, with its vertiginous steps, hanging terraces and yew parlour – those 'dark, secret rooms of yew hiding in the slope of the valley', as Sackville-West put it; another writer once compared it to the setting for *The Secret Garden*. Thanks to Lady Mander's ministrations, blue irises, wallflowers, peonies and Granny's Bonnet are in full flower by early summer, along with foxglove and clematis in shades of violet and mauve. By the church, mosaics of roses and trailing lilies hang amid the conifers. Behind the manor, beyond the yew, holly and walnut trees, lies the cool sanctuary of the beech woods; in the spring, bluebells and wild garlic form a delicate carpet.

As befits a storybook valley, Owlpen is a sanctuary for birds (sparrowhawks, buzzards and ravens) and animals (badgers, foxes and roe deer). The meadow opposite the manor house, known as the Great Mead, harbours protected butterflies and wild flowers. Rare orchids and the distinctive, bell-shaped pasque flower, which blooms at Easter, add to the air of enchantment. If you linger past twilight, when a mystical aura seeps in, you may witness the eerie spectacle of a glow-worm colony.

With its secret garden and Arts and Crafts design, the old manor house has a storybook feel.

No wonder *Country Life* journalist Christopher Hussey, writing in the 1950s, concluded that Owlpen was nothing less than 'a dream made real'. Fortunately, the passage of time has done nothing to diminish that charisma.

OTHER BEAUTY SPOTS

For fine vistas coupled with archaeological wonder, Uley Bury is an Iron Age hill fort with far-reaching westward views over the Severn Vale towards the Welsh mountains. On the same ancient theme, Hetty Pegler's Tump is a 4,000-year-old long barrow complete with Neolithic burial chambers, just north of Owlpen.

Painswick, north-east of Owlpen, was once a wealthy wool town. Today, it's a less touristy Cotswold alternative to Broadway, Bourton and Burford, but arguably more lovely, with its steep, twisting streets, grey limestone buildings and sleepy churchyard that is shaded by mature yews. Legend has it that if more than 99 trees are allowed to grow there, the Devil will appear; another counters this by claiming that the trees are uncountable. The Rococo Garden, outside the town, recreates the flamboyance and frivolity of early 18th-century garden design.

The Slad Valley, south of Painswick, was once home to the writer Laurie Lee, and the inspiration for his classic memoir, *Cider with Rosie*, a sepia-tinted paean to Cotswold village life in the period after World War I. Decades on, it remains a tranquil rural setting in which to while away an afternoon with a picnic – or a pint of cider at the Woolpack pub.

WHERE TO STAY & EAT

Owlpen is even more romantic and atmospheric by night. Deep in the valley, it gets pitch-dark and pin-drop quiet – and easy to believe in the three resident ghosts. You might even encounter them if you stay in one of the nine quaint and comfortable estate cottages (01453 860261, www.owlpen.com).

Alternatively, the Amberley Inn (01453 872565, www.theamberley.co.uk), close to Stroud, blends tradition – cosy fires, beamed ceilings, four-poster beds – with contemporary flair. It also boasts views over the valley of Woodchester, where the Romans created the Orpheus mosaic, the second-largest of its kind in Europe, in 325 AD (the original lies buried in a churchyard; a replica can be seen at nearby Prinknash Abbey).

At the Bell in Sapperton (01285 760298, www.foodatthebell.co.uk), top-quality, locally sourced ingredients – South Cerney goat's cheese, Old Spot pork, free-range Newent chicken – crowd the menu.

Painswick's St Michael's House (01452 814555, www.stmichaelsrestaurant.co.uk), also an elegant B&B, overlooks the village's famous, yew-filled churchyard. The 17th-century building, less than an hour from Owlpen, houses a sophisticated restaurant that uses locally sourced ingredients in its fusion dishes (fennel and pernod soup, jellied chicken livers with pear chutney).

Owlpen's own Cyder House restaurant can be found in the rustic Great Barn adjoining the main house (01453 860816, www.owlpen.com), but both venues are shut for refurbishment in 2010 (note: the garden remains open, call for times).

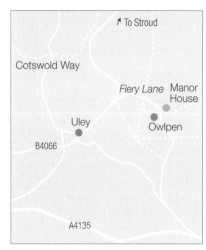

HOW TO GET THERE

Owlpen is 12 miles south of Gloucester near the village of Uley. **By car** It is 10 miles from Junctions 13 and 14 on the M5, and 12 miles from Junction 18 of the M4, via the A46. The B4066 goes to Uley. When the house is open (*see right*), you can park nearby. Otherwise, park in Uley and walk. **By train** The nearest train station to Owlpen is Cam and Dursley, six miles away (National Rail Enquiries, 08457 484950). **On foot** The village of Uley at the top of Fiery Lane is a good base for walks on the country footpaths, including those through the woods towards Nympsfield and Uley Bury, past the manor house along the Ewelme; and close to the remains of the Victorian estate. The Ewelme path is reached through a metal 'squeeze-belly' stile on Fiery Lane. The manor house gardens are open Tue, Thur and Sun (2-5pm) in spring and summer. **Map** Ordnance Survey Explorer 168, Stroud, Tetbury and Malmesbury; grid ref ST799984.

FURTHER REFERENCE

Nailsworth Tourist Information Centre (01453 839222, www.cotswolds.info). Owlpen Manor (01453 860816, www.owlpen.com).

North Meadow

Flower power.

At first sight, North Meadow doesn't look much different from the land around it. This is border country between Wiltshire and Gloucestershire, and it doesn't have the chocolate-box prettiness of the Cotswolds, to the north, nor the sumptuous glossiness of the Wessex downs to the south. And yet every year there's a steady pilgrimage of interested parties to an expanse of open grassland near the town of Cricklade.

North Meadow's pilgrims have done their research, because the attraction of this 108-acre traditional hay field is not immediately obvious; if you choose the wrong time of year, you might wonder what all the fuss is about. Get it right, though, and you will be surprised at how many entranced hours can be spent in a simple hay meadow, staring at a botanical spectacle – a sea of snakeshead fritillaries, one of Britain's rarest wild flowers.

The fritillaries have put the nearby town of Cricklade on the map. Founded in the 9th century by the Saxons, it is now expanded by housing estates, filled with commuters who work in Swindon. But Cricklade's core is still handsome in yellow Cotswold stone, with a couple of old coaching inns and a fine line in hanging baskets and floral displays.

Cricklade is also the first town of any significance on the Thames, which at this point is somewhere between toddler and teenager in riverine terms, being only eight miles from its source. Like most juveniles, the young Thames can get quite stroppy at this stage in its development, and after periods of heavy rain, it sprawls right across the meadow like a teenager on a sofa.

In other parts of the country, such unruly behaviour would have long since been restrained, for the sake of agricultural productivity, but the keepers of North Meadow are happy to let the temperamental Thames have its time-honoured moods. A regular winter flooding is one of the reasons why this continues to be one of the UK's most flower-rich meadows, and one of the reasons why it hosts, in particular, around 80 per cent of the population of the snakeshead fritillary.

Every year, usually from early April until early May, some 1.5 million of these purple flowers raise their delicate heads among the coarse grasses of North Meadow. Roughly bell-shaped, snakeskin-mottled, and ankle high, they tinkle silently in the breeze, carpeting the Meadow in a floating purple haze of pixie hats. It's a visual treat, and you don't have to be a botanist to fall under their spell; but it is important to know quite how such delicate organisms have managed to cling so obstinately to this patch of ground.

The secret lies in the land management, for this is a Lammas Meadow, common ground that was originally gifted to the inhabitants of Cricklade during the reign of Charles I, and which escaped the various Enclosure Acts of the 19th century. The Meadow, and its grazing rights, were administered by a Manorial Court Leet, a rare form of local government that still exists in Cricklade today, and still manages the Meadow in the same way it always did. Put simply, thanks to its status, the land has sidestepped the agricultural 'improvement' that has destroyed the original floral diversity of most of Britain's farmland. And now that it is a reserve owned by English Nature, it looks set to remain 'unimproved' until kingdom come.

The Meadow's system is simple and traditional. The Court Leet appoints a Hayward, who supervises the grazing and upkeep of the Meadow and collects the fees that are due. The grazing is let from 12 August to 12 February, usually for around 25 horses, for the princely sum of £1.25 per head. The rest of the year, the Meadow is left to its own devices, right up until July, when the hay is finally cut.

This cycle is perfectly suited to fritillaries, whose shoots first break through the soil just after the horses have been removed in late February. Initially, the flower's unopened viper's head lies along the ground, until the vigour of spring raises it aloft. Thereafter, the fritillaries remain unmolested through their blooming cycle, before seeding in July, just before haymaking. And they have a unique method of dispersal, too, with the seed pod generating a little burst of heat that attracts bumble bees.

Not that there are fritillaries all over North Meadow. For much of the 108 acres it is the common or garden dandelion that shrieks 'look at me, look at me', while cuckoo flowers and the occasional clump of marsh marigold also compete for attention. The fritillaries tend to concentrate on the northern flank up against the river Churn, particularly in an area known as the Garden. Here, too, there's a significant proportion of the minority white fritillaries, highly noticeable among the purples, although they only represent 11 per cent of the overall population.

The only recent disturbance to North Meadow's ecology came during the war, when the size of the open space aroused fears that the Germans could land here, so giant concrete blocks were laid out to stop planes from landing. These days, some weathered stones are still visible, but these are historic boundary-markers dating from the time when Cricklade's households had their own allocation of hay.

Of course, there's good reason to come here outside the fritillary season, too. From June onwards, rich purple greater burnet and common knapweed dominate, contrasting

Clockwise from top left: cuckoo flowers, seen in close-up and in the field, flourish in traditional hay meadows; the snakeshead fritillary is the star of the show; a historic hay lot boundary marker.

with the yellows of meadow buttercup and yellow rattle. Elsewhere in the Meadow, there'll be ox-eye daisies, meadow rue and meadowsweet.

And then there are the human species, for the Meadow is well used at all times of the year. The Thames path runs along the southern flank beside the teenage river, where it is lined with willow, hawthorn and blackthorn trees. Dog-walking, child-running, and kite-flying are all widely practised here, although visitors are encouraged to keep to the network of paths. The only thing that is discouraged here is interfering with the plants. If you arrived with a spade, you would be unlikely to dig for long, for the inhabitants of Cricklade are very proud of their Lammas Meadow and its unique flower show.

OTHER BEAUTY SPOTS

The village-dotted Vale of Pewsey, due south of Swindon between Devises and Pewsey, is archetypal English countryside, a fertile valley protected by the long ridge of the Marlborough Downs, with the Kennet and Avon canal wandering unhurriedly through. Reeds and water lilies fringe the banks; ducks and moorhens nibble the weeds and anglers

The River Thames is virtually a trickle in North Meadow; its source is only eight miles upstream.

nibble their sandwiches. In days when canals were important transport arteries, the Kennet and Avon was pretty busy here, but now just about the only thing that passes is time.

To the west of Swindon stands the Westonbirt Arboretum, the most outstanding collection of native and exotic trees in Europe. Established in 1829, it now has 18,000 trees and shrubs in more than 300 species spread across 600 acres. The ground is sandy loam, and is so tree-friendly that many of the species – maples, whitebeams and Caucasian oaks – are the largest in Britain. It is carefully landscaped with 17 miles of footpath, and is one of the best places in the UK to see autumn colours, thanks to its growing collection of maples, the stalwart of fall colours in New England and Eastern Canada.

WHERE TO STAY & EAT

The Fritillary Tea Room, situated in a converted chapel by the Thames bridge on the way out of Cricklade towards North Meadow, is a community effort, and known for its bread-and-butter pudding. Staffed by volunteer organisations, and only open from 10am to 5pm on weekends during the fritillary season (usually throughout April), it also has informative displays about North Meadow along the walls. For more information see www.cricklade inbloom.co.uk/north_meadow.html.

For the rest of the year, the Red Lion Inn (01793 750776, www.theredlioncricklade. co.uk) on Cricklade High Street is a traditional British pub dating from the 1600s, with a pleasant garden at the back, and a food menu that has embraced gastropub principles. The Red Lion also has five spotless guest rooms, in a style that is balanced between traditional and contemporary.

For a more rural setting, and more luxurious accommodation, Cricklade Hotel and Country Club (01793 750751, www.crickladehotel.co.uk) sits in 30 acres of grounds, with its own golf course, spa and indoor swimming pool. A popular location for weddings, the hotel is a conversion of a 100-year-old country house, and has a Victorian-style conservatory running the length of the building on the sunnier, south-facing side. Some of the rooms have four-poster beds and views across the Wiltshire Downs.

HOW TO GET THERE

North Meadow is in north Wiltshire near Cricklade, halfway between Swindon and Cirencester. **By road** Cricklade is on the A419. To reach North Meadow, follow the high street north out of town across the river bridge; the meadow entrance is 600 feet beyond the bridge on the left, with parking along the road's verges. **By train** Swindon is the nearest station (National Rail Enquiries, 08457 484950). **By bus** From Swindon, buses 51, 51A, 52 and 53 run to Cricklade. The 51 (01793 521415, www.stagecoachbus.com) is the most regular service, with buses leaving once an hour Mon-Sat. **On foot** It takes about 45 minutes to walk the meadow. The biggest concentration of fritillaries are in a part of the meadow called 'the Garden' on the north-east side, a ten-minute walk from the entry. The Thames Path runs across the south side of the meadow. During peak fritillary season – about the second week of April to early May – a small marquee is set up for enquiries and tours. **Map** Ordnance Survey Explorer 169, Cirencester & Swindon; grid ref SU094945.

FURTHER REFERENCE

For updates on the state of the fritillaries, contact the warden on 07795 316191 or see www.crickladeinbloom.co.uk/ north_meadow.html. The warden, along with representatives from the Court Leet, lead free guided walks during the season. Swindon Tourist Information (01793 530328, www.visitwiltshire.co.uk). See also www.naturalengland.org.uk.

Savernake Forest

Special branches.

Deep in the heart of civilised Wiltshire, on the meandering road between Hungerford and Marlborough, the lush, open fields of this rich farming county gradually give way to darkness as overhanging trees encroach on the side of the road, and signs warn drivers to slow down for stray deer. Step off the tarmac and on to the forest's ferny floor, and body and mind are soon engulfed in an ethereal world where twisted branches take on epic proportions and the crack of twigs echoes the fairy footsteps of Peaseblossom and Puck. Welcome to the Savernake Forest, Europe's oldest planted woodland and home to around 2,600 oaks and 2,400 beeches. This is ancient woodland like no other, more than 1,000 years old in parts and worthy of a mention in the Domesday Book.

The star of the show is the Big Belly Oak, also known as the decanter oak because of its bulbous shape. A little green plaque denotes its claim to fame: it was one of the 50 trees honoured by the Tree Council to mark the Queen's Golden Jubilee in 2002, and if age is any mark of greatness, then this well-rounded, 1,100-year-old oak thoroughly deserves its place in the sylvan pantheon. Big Belly Oak is easy to reach from Marlborough's well-manicured high street. The A346 climbs sharply out of the town up to Postern Hill, the forest's highest point, and the ancient oak comes into view about a mile later, on the edge of the road, with an iron belt around its girth like some metal cummerbund vainly attempting to hold in the bulging barky stomach above. This is no fashionable accoutrement, though – in 2001, the tree was in danger of splitting in two and the belt now keeps it together, and off the busy main road.

Unfortunately, another ancient Savernake oak, the handsomely named Duke's Vaunt – located far deeper in the forest and a challenge to even find, let alone care for – was not so lucky. It was once hollow and some 30 feet in diameter. In the 18th century, it made the ultimate tree house, complete with a door and lock, and was capable of 'sheltering 20 choir boys' within its mighty trunk, according to a Saxon document. But now it stands forlorn – or rather sits, as the split down the middle has deposited most of its trunk on the forest floor – like a gnarled old man surrounded by tall, sprightly conifers.

Duke's Vaunt and Big Belly are just two of the Savernake's great 'monarch' oaks. Others in the 4,500-acre forest include the King of Limbs, Spider Oak and Old Paunchy and Slingsby. Running through the middle of this majestic growth is the Grand Avenue, a dead straight road that starts outside Marlborough and emerges five miles later near Grade I-listed Tottenham House, formerly a 100-room estate pile, now a luxury country house hotel (the current estate owner, the Earl of Cardigan, resides deep in the forest at Savernake

Savernake Forest has 2,600 oak trees, including the 1,100-year-old Big Belly Oak (next page). Ailesbury Column (right) was brought in from London by the estate owners in 1781.

Lodge). Laid out by Lancelot 'Capability' Brown during the 1700s, the beech-lined Grand Avenue is, at four miles, the longest avenue in the country. Plum in the middle of it is Eight Walks, a stately junction where six other landscaped drives lead off into the undergrowth.

Beyond the ordered 18th-century avenues of Capability Brown, and the ordured 20th-century picnic areas of Postern Hill, the deep forest seems impenetrable, and it can be tempting to stick to the tarmacked 'trunk road' of the Grand Avenue. But the real wonders of the woods lie beyond the landscaping. For a good half-day clomp, park at Hat Gate, a mile south of Big Belly Oak, and wander back northwards through leafy woodland until you reach an old milestone at the entrance to Charcoal Burners Road. Down this leafy track, a derelict building stands as testament to the Savernake's World War II role as a vast ammunition dump.

This southern half of the forest contains more ancient mixed woodland than the northern half, and as a result is rich in wildlife. The trees resound with hawfinch,

woodpeckers and nightjars, and the forest floor hosts roe, muntjac and fallow deer. Just south of the milestone, a path leads to a beautiful clearing, at the centre of which stands the Oak Cluster, becalmed in a sea of wildflowers and ferns. These are not the most spectacular or oldest trees in the forest, but there is a wonderful sense of tranquillity here. Following the track south-east, one comes upon Bitham Pool, one of 20 small pools in the forest; further on, carpets of bluebells burst forth in late April and early May (nearby West Woods is a sea of purple). The path ends at Ailesbury Column, an incongruous 100-feet tall Ionic column topped with an elaborate urn. The column was a capital cast-off, having stood for the first 20 years of its life in Hammersmith, West London, before the estate owners transplanted it to the forest 230 years ago for added grandeur.

Indeed, the human history of the Savernake Forest is almost as fascinating as the trees that inhabit it. William the Conqueror gave the domain to one of his knights who had fought at the Battle of Hastings in 1066, and since then it has remained in the same family for 31 generations. Its historic heyday came about in the 16th century, when Sir John Seymour, then head of the estate family, would entertain the great and the good for a spot of deer hunting. During one of these sporting forays, shortly after the execution of Anne Boleyn in 1536, King Henry VIII stayed with Sir John and bagged rather more than he came for. The king fell for Sir John's daughter, Jane, and the couple were subsequently married. As historians know, Jane's great claim to fame was that she gave the King what he so badly wanted – a son. Jane died in childbirth, but not before producing a future king, Edward VI, whose short, six-year reign ended when he died at the tender age of 15. But his spirit lives on in this most regal of rural retreats.

OTHER BEAUTY SPOTS

Magnificent bluebell carpets blanket West Woods, four miles west of Savernake Forest, in glorious technicolor during late April and early May.

The Avebury stone circle, also west of Savernake Forest and partly encompassing the pretty village of Avebury, is one of Europe's most arresting Neolithic sites, and the largest stone circle in Britain. But size isn't everything: the truly magical thing about Avebury compared to, say, Stonehenge, is that you can roam where you like and get up close and personal with Neolithic man. The main circle is roughly a quarter of a mile across, with two smaller circles within. The whole ancient site is surrounded by a steep ditch and bank.

Even more striking than Avebury is the curious grassy mound of Silbury Hill, two miles away on the A4 Bath road. At 100 feet high and 500 feet wide, it's the largest man-made mound in Europe and was probably built around 2,800 BC. Its purpose, though, is unclear – religious monument, ancient burial chamber, Neolithic reservoir, alien creation? In this county of mythical menhirs and baffling crop circles, history is thickly laced with mystery.

WHERE TO STAY & EAT

The Red Lion pub in the middle of Avebury (01672 539266) is no gastropub star, but the location makes up for it – where else can you sup a pint of ale on a bench in the middle of a 4,000-year-old stone circle?

Nearby Marlborough is a handsome market town with a famous public school and a wide high street marred by chain restaurants. The Food Gallery (01672 514069, www. thefoodgallery.co.uk) serves the best local coffee, along with home-made cakes, salads, soups and sandwiches. For more formal fare, Coles (01672 515004, www.coles restaurant.co.uk) has an ambitious Modern European menu and a candlelit dining room. The three-star Castle & Ball (01672 515201, www.castleandball.com) hotel dates from the 16th century, and is a cosy place with 35 bedrooms and plenty of rustic timbers.

The one Michelin-starred Harrow Inn in the pretty village of Little Bedwyn (01672 870871, www.harrowinn.co.uk) is the area's standout restaurant. Dishes such as caramelised belly of Kelmscott pork or grilled fillet of Welsh black beef with horseradish potato cake are executed with aplomb, and the wine list is superb. Booking essential. Afterwards, bed down nearby at the excellent White House B&B (01672 870321, www. the-white-house-b-and-b.co.uk). The former vicarage has a photogenic garden that borders the Kennet and Avon Canal, and two homely bedrooms.

← To Marlborough
A4
Grand Avenue
A346
● Big Belly Oak
Old Milestone ●
Oak Cluster ●
Charcoal Burners Road
Bitham Pool
🅿 Ailesbury Column

HOW TO GET THERE

The 4,500-acre Savernake Forest is half a mile south-east of Marlborough. **By road** Follow the M4 till J14, then the A338 to Hungerford, and the A4 to Marlborough. Two main roads skirt the forest: the A4 and the A346. The four-mile Grand Avenue, a tarmacked road accessible to cars, bisects the forest. There are two official car parks in or near the forest, both off the A346 Marlborough-to-Burbage road. The largest is at Postern Hill, which also has barbecue facilities and a campsite (www. forestry.gov.uk). The Big Belly Oak is half a mile south of Postern Hill on the edge of the A346. **By train** The nearest station is Bedwyn, two miles away (National Rail Enquiries, 08457 484950). **By bus** There are regular buses (0871 200 2233, www.traveline.org.uk) between Bedwyn station and Marlborough, with a stop at Forest Hill (ideal for access to the forest). **On foot** There are plenty of walking trails, but a map is essential. The tourist information centre in Marlborough sells maps and walk pamphlets. **Map Ordnance Survey** Explorer 157, Marlborough & Savernake Forest; grid ref SU225665.

FURTHER REFERENCE

There are tourist information centres in Marlborough (01672 512663) and Avebury (01672 539179), or go to www.visitwiltshire.co.uk. See also www.savernakeestate.co.uk and the Forestry Commission (01672 512520. www.forestry.gov.uk).

Thames Valley

The river mild.

Beyond the hubbub of London and the suburbs of Reading, the character of the River Thames changes. In contrast to the well-known tidal and towny portions, these western rural reaches offer a gentle beauty. There are more thrillingly wild corners of England, and landscapes that are more spectacular. But you'd be hard-pushed to pinpoint a more quintessentially English patch than this stretch of river, which runs through the rolling countryside of Berkshire and Oxfordshire. There's a serene and bucolic air to this middle section, roughly halfway between the river's source in the Cotswolds and its bracing Essex estuary, and bounded by the villages of Pangbourne and Dorchester. Cutting its way through chalky downland, buttercup-laden water meadows grazed by cattle and, at one point, a dramatic Chilterns gorge, this is a rich patchwork of green and very pleasant countryside.

Not just a pretty face, however, this stretch of the Thames played a vital role in the nation's history as an arterial transport route. Farm settlements sprang up along the Thames Valley during the 16th and 17th centuries in order to feed London. Barges plied the waters between Oxford and the capital, laden with food, livestock and timber. But with the arrival of rail and motorways, the river became a place of calm and picturesque beauty, of pleasure boats and dainty picnics on its banks – an image bolstered by Jerome K Jerome's comic novel *Three Men in a Boat*, published in 1889. Thanks to strict greenbelt planning laws, the river between Reading and Oxford is virtually the same soothing idyll that it was for Jerome in the 19th century. On lazy, hazy summer days, pleasure-seekers still drift along the river on rented boats. Picnics are still in evidence too, particularly downstream near the sophisticated delights of Cookham, Marlow and Henley-on-Thames.

Walkers can trace the river's twists and turns on the Thames Path. To start, a dainty latticework bridge crosses the Thames at Pangbourne, linking Berkshire and Oxfordshire. In the latter, on the north bank, the quietly genteel village of Whitchurch-on-Thames is a pleasing departure point for a waterside walk. Here, high up on a chalky Chiltern cliff, there are tantalising snippets of river glimpsed through the beech woods. The forest's dusty, olive-green hues complement the emerald water meadows; in autumn, the copper and golden trees are similarly striking against the river's grey-green backdrop. After its lofty beginning, the path drops down to the river a mile upstream, ducking under one of Brunel's Great Western railway bridges, and out into the gorgeous Goring Gap.

The narrowest part of the Thames Valley, the Gap is a geological talking point, dividing the wooded hills of the Berkshire Downs from the more jagged peaks of the Chilterns; it was carved out by the Thames during the Ice Age, seemingly formed by the river's determination to find a way to the sea. Down by the tow path, fields border the river into Goring, a tidy Edwardian village. Across a timber bridge, Goring's sister village, Streatley, lies on the Berkshire side, where the landscape becomes more rolling and rural and the path hugs the river. It's easy to fall in love with this particular stretch of the Thames: the river meanders gently along, bordered by graceful weeping willows, tall ashes and sedge grasses; in summer, the profusion of greens is speckled with the purples of thistle, willow herb and loosestrife, and the busy whites, yellows and blues of bumble bees, butterflies and dragonflies. At times, the river has a powerful, magnetic presence, its silence broken only by the plaintive squeak of a coot or moorhen, or the drone of insects darting over the surface of the water. Even when it's out of sight, one can feel the river sweeping past – and catch wafts of its rich muddy tang. At dawn, mist clings to the sides of the valley and the water cuts a still, glassy path through the quiet land.

The river's hypnotic, languid beauty stretches all the way up to Oxford – some 36 miles or so from Pangbourne. But the slumbering village of Moulsford is a reasonable goal for walkers who start out the day in Whitchurch. For a panoramic finale, however, energetic hikers may want to press on for the Wittenham Clumps, further north near the ancient abbey village of Dorchester. On the south bank near Little Wittenham, and capped with beech copses, these two bizarre hillocks, also known as Lady Dunch's buttocks, are a geological mystery amid such modest terrain, and were once the setting of an Iron Age fort. They offer sweeping views across a bend in the river to Dorchester Abbey and the undulating Oxfordshire countryside beyond. Looking down – and away from Didcot Power Station – one feels thankful that this scene hasn't changed much since those three men and their boat ended their journey here a century ago.

OTHER BEAUTY SPOTS

Tipping out into the Thames at Pangbourne, the River Pang is a chalk stream that flows south-east through isolated valleys in the Berkshire Downs. Like Mole, prepare to be 'bewitched, entranced and fascinated' by the river that was Kenneth Grahame's inspiration for *The Wind in the Willows*. Passing through farmland for most of its 25-mile journey to the Thames, the Pang has retained its natural beauty, in spite of the beady-eyed property developers who hover (nearby Theale and Pangbourne are commuter towns). Parts of the

A sleepy stretch of the Thames between Goring and Basildon.

river and valley that Grahame visited have been designated a conservation area (Moor Copse nature reserve, near the villages Tidmarsh and Sulham), in an attempt to encourage Ratty's descendants – now more politely referred to as water voles – to return to the river. Head further upstream still, and the river becomes ever more enchanting as it winds through wheat fields, ancient woods and such picture-book villages as Stanford Dingley and Bucklebury.

A neolithic nexus, ancient Streatley is where the Thames meets the Ridgeway. The latter is a prehistoric route, now a National Trail, which starts 85 miles to the west in Avebury in Wiltshire and follows a chalk downland ridge to the top of Streatley Hill. There, with

expansive views of the Thames to the east, Lardon Chase and Lough Down (owned by the National Trust) form one of the largest areas of untouched chalk grassland in the county and a Site of Special Scientific Interest (SSSI) that protects wild flowers and rare butterflies. Further west, on the Oxfordshire section of the Ridgeway, mystical sights abound: there are several Neolithic and Iron Age settlements, including the mysterious Wayland's Smithy, Uffington Castle and the iconic White Horse, which was cut into the hill 3,000 years ago.

WHERE TO STAY & EAT

The Beetle and Wedge (01491 651381, www.beetleandwedge.co.uk) was once a boathouse and hotel, but is now a B&B with river-view rooms, huge bathtubs and simple, light and airy decor. The old boathouse is now a decent, if slightly pricey, restaurant serving traditional fish and meat dishes from its charcoal grill, as well as a more adventurous shellfish and game menu.

John Barleycorn (01491 872509, www.thejohnbarleycornpub.co.uk), a cosy 17th-century village pub in Goring on Thames, has three small but attractive rooms (all with spruce, clean bathrooms). Less aspirational than the Beetle and Wedge, the pub menu does the classics (ploughman's lunch, steak and kidney pie), as well as an excellent pint of Brakspear's ale. A short walk down nearby Ferry Lane (where Oscar Wilde wrote parts of *An Ideal Husband* at Ferry Cottage) leads to the Thames Path.

Fyfield Manor (01491 835184, www.fyfieldmanor.co.uk), a venerable country pile outside the village of Benson, is purportedly the oldest building in Oxfordshire. Though its

The quaint and genteel village of Whitchurch-on-Thames (left); the chalk grassland in the Thames Valley is rich in wild flowers.

origins are 12th century, the environmentally friendly Cloisters building is a new addition, with comfortable rooms, big bathrooms and organic breakfasts. The gardens have streams where water vole loll on the banks.

This stretch of the Thames is sprinkled with pubs. In the heart of the Berkshire Downs, the Bell Inn (01635 578272) is beloved of walkers and real-ale fans (it serves Kingsdown and Arkells). Run by the same family for 250 years, it dates from the 13th century. The Pot Kiln (01635 201366, www.potkiln.org), in Frilsham, was originally built to feed and water the workers at the nearby brick kiln. Today, it's a charming spot to sup West Berkshire ales, scoff fine, locally sourced food (confit belly pork, Linkenholt Estate roe deer) and befriend the nosy cows grazing in front of you.

HOW TO GET THERE

Pangbourne is 50 miles west of London and 25 miles south of Oxford. Dorchester is 10 miles south of Oxford. **By road** The M4 and M40 are the nearest motorways. For Pangbourne, get off at junction 12 (Theale) and follow the A340 for two miles. Whitchurch-on-Thames is across the bridge on the other side of the river. For Dorchester, take the M40, B4009 and then A4047. **By train** Pangbourne, Goring and Streatley rail stations. There are direct trains from London (National Rail Enquiries, 08457 484950). **By bus** Buses are scarce. Dorchester is not on the train line, but there are sporadic bus services (Mon-Fri) from Oxford and Wallingford with Thames Travel (08712 002233, www.thames-travel.co.uk). Thames Travel has five buses a day (Mon-Sat) from Wallingford to Pangbourne. **On foot** The Thames Path and Ridgeway walks are easy to follow. **By bicycle** Mountain High (Pangbourne, 01189 841851, www.mountainhigh.co.uk). **By boat** Caversham Boat Services (Frys Island, Reading, 0118 957 4323, www. cavershamboatservices.co.uk) rent out narrow boats, cabin cruisers and rowing boats. Benson Waterfront (01491 838304, www.bensonwaterfront.com) rent out cabin cruisers. Thames Canoes (01628 478787, www.thamescanoes. co.uk) will drop you off and pick you up from various points on the river. **Map** Ordnance Survey Explorer 171, Chiltern Hills West; grid reference SU602808.

FURTHER REFERENCE

Newbury (01635 30267, www.visitwest berkshire.org), Goring-on-Thames (01491 873565) and Wallingford (01491 826972, www.wallingfordtown.com) have tourist information centres. See www.national trail.co.uk, www.ridgewayfriends.org.uk/ path.html, www.thames-path.org.uk.

The Thames near Pangbourne – a perfect place to start a walk along the river.

Burnham Beeches

Golden oldies.

Bankers, bless their money-hungry little hearts. When they snatched Burnham Beeches from the jaws of redevelopment 120 years ago, in a bid for good PR, they bequeathed us one of the most glorious nature reserves in south-east England. It's a vital lung for a choking capital, and the largest surviving slice of prehistoric beech woodland that once covered Buckinghamshire. And they did so just in time. What began as uncivilised wildwood, millennia old and teeming with cutthroats and highwaymen, had been gradually chopped into chair legs in the name of progress. Over centuries, the woods were tamed and developed; they now survive only in accidental pockets squeezed in between farmland, suburban sprawl and the gated mansions of the Home Counties rich list. But at Burnham, you can still feel the primeval energy of an ancient place: the breath of the forest touching your skin.

What possessed the Corporation of London to buy Burnham Beeches and present it to the nation? The financial hotshots who commute from the area today might have recognised the crisis faced by the bankers back in 1880, when overstretched and undermonitored banks collapsed into heaps of ruinous debt. But Victorian spin doctors recast the City as a champion of the little people and a defender of the countryside in the face of rapacious developers, whose rows of cheap terraces were marching unstoppably outward and threatening England's idylls. Snapping up pieces of greenery – not just Burnham, but Queen's Wood in Highgate, Epping Forest, Ashstead Common and, more recently, Hampstead Heath – was a masterstroke of philanthropic rebranding for the City.

Clocking in at – appropriately – a rough square mile, Burnham Beeches is not huge, and nor is it wild. You're too close to London for ruggedness to survive; the landscape is tended, and on main paths, actually tarmacked. But there's still the distinct possibility of magic in the air. Off the beaten tracks, the tree canopy closes around you and dappled pathways veined with roots dip and weave into forgotten places. Here, the stately full-grown beeches are a green cathedral roofed with far-off dancing leaves, the space inside sighing with a reverential hush. In autumn, the golden foliage is a blaze of glory, and crisp orange bracken tops the rain-dark earth.

For all that, the real stars of the show at Burnham are the old pollards, some dating back 450 years. These 'very reverend vegetables' (as the poet Thomas Gray put it, rather oddly, in a letter to Horace Walpole in 1737) are beeches that were pruned for generations in the traditional manner, cut back each year to human height, allowing foresters to harvest a new flush of straight young branches every season. Over time, trees treated in this way develop peculiar habits, morphing into strange, bulbous forms

From spring buds to autumn foliage, Burnham Beeches is photogenic throughout the year; many of the characterful pollarded trees date back 450 years.

sprouting skewed, chunky limbs. Depending on the light, the time of year or your natural disposition, their sculptural forms are either eerie or comical or sad. Sometimes, the pollards seem to hunch malevolently, ready to grab at you, like the evil forest Dorothy passed through on her way to Oz; at other times, they are the kind of shaggy, nonsensical creatures drawn by Dr Seuss. Mostly, their smooth grey trunks and rounded protuberances conjure images of elephants or sea lions, friendly and sympathetically ugly in a way that the disdainful oaks, with their defensive crocodilian bark, can never be.

Leaflets in the visitors' centre exhort us to leave the pollards alone – they house a variety of precious beetles – but it's hard not to touch them gently in a kind of silent greeting. Their human scale endows them with a companionable air and their hollow centres, scoured out by fungi and weather and insects, invite us over their thresholds – and induce goosebumps. Getting too personal with these twisted beasts tends to rouse a deep-buried superstitious reflex, summoning Ovidian nightmares or horror-movie clichés. Not for nothing do folk tales make such places the doorway into fairyland; not for nothing have neo-pagans and conspiracy theorists been reeled in by the wood's spooky charms. Back in the 1960s, you couldn't move for would-be warlocks rustling about in the undergrowth near a gnarled 800-year-old specimen known as Druid's Oak.

In the end, it's nature, not the supernatural, that thrives here. As well as the invertebrates that make the Beeches a designated Site of Special Scientific Interest – say hello to the *Ischnomera sanguinicollis* beetle and the *Limax tenellus* wood slug – you can twitch for sparrowhawks, redstarts, nightjars and nightingales, or spot rare dormice, moths and butterflies. Along with the famous beeches, there are oaks, hazel, birch and pine trees; honeysuckle, bluebells and wood anemones. Heathered heaths support rare junipers and a chain of bogs and ponds, valuable habitats for hard-to-find mosses and rushes.

It's a delicate ecosystem, and maintaining it takes money. There's a 500-year plan to coax neglected pollards back to health and create a new generation. Urgent research into climate change is going on here, and ambitious sustainability targets that aim to turn the Beeches back into a proper working woodland, complete with grazing animals and saleable timber. Volunteers help out, but it is the knowledgeable staff that keeps the place in prime condition. Luckily, the Corporation of London has deep pockets. Say what you like about capitalism: those top-hatted Victorian financiers and their splendid banking crisis did Britain proud with Burnham Beeches.

OTHER BEAUTY SPOTS

Spreading over 5,000 lovely acres, Windsor Great Park was once the private hunting ground of the royal family, and parts of it are now open to the public, including a deer park, the three-mile Long Walk and the Royal Landscape. This last section encompasses the Savill Garden (contemporary and classic design), the Valley Gardens (a flowering forest) and Virginia Water Lake (with temples, follies and a totem pole).

Dating back to the late Bronze Age, White Horse Hill is an ancient figure carved into the side of the chalk hill at Uffington. It is part of a complex of ancient monuments, including 'Uffington Castle' (actually an Iron Age hill fort), Dragon Hill (an odd-looking mound with a bare top, said to be where St George killed the dragon) and a Neolithic long barrow known as Wayland's Smithy. Set on the Ridgeway, Britain's oldest road, this is an atmospheric, windswept place, even more impressive in winter than in summer.

Near Burnham, Hedgerley is the kind of picture-postcard village that its neighbour just isn't. A winner of Buckingham's best village award, it has a gorgeous Victorian church nestled among sheep, a lovely pond, an RSPB reserve and miles of footpaths.

WHERE TO STAY & EAT

Cliveden House Hotel (01628 668561, www.clivedenhouse.co.uk) is an Italianate stately home designed by Sir Charles 'Houses of Parliament' Barry in 1851. Bought by the Astors in 1893, it was immortalised in the 1960s as the place where John Profumo had his ill-fated liaison with Christine Keeler. It's currently a five-star hotel stuffed with gilded panelling, rich carving and chandeliers, and once boasted 'the world's most expensive sandwich' on its menu. Rooms are named after famous guests from Cliveden's past,

Pine trees complement the famous beeches, along with oak, birch and hazel.

(Gladstone, Kipling, Chaplin). The bill for a night's accommodation starts at £250, but you can stroll in the stunning gardens for £7.50 (they are owned by the National Trust).

Set amid manicured gardens, the 18th-century Burnham Beeches Hotel (0870 609 6124, www.corushotels.com) oozes Georgian elegance. The large, chic rooms are done up in neutral tones, and there is starched linen in the formal dining room.

The Chequers Inn (01628 529575, www.chequers-inn.com) is a family-run, 17th-century coaching inn on a country lane. The restaurant looks swish, but the prices for the classic, English-French cuisine are moderate, and it also holds barbecues in its garden in good weather. You can stay here, too, in one of 17 old English-style rooms.

The Jolly Woodman (01753 644350, www.thejollywoodman.co.uk) in Littleworth Common is a hidden woodland gem. The 19th-century pub offers real ales, hearty cooking, a nice garden and a child-friendly atmosphere. The White Horse in Hedgerley (01753 643225) is another country charmer: housed in a 500-year-old building, this rustic pub serves home-made food and real ales amid beams and exposed brickwork.

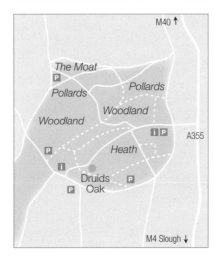

HOW TO GET THERE

Burnham Beeches lies north of Slough and south of Beaconsfield in the county of Buckinghamshire. **By road** Take the M4 or M40, then the A355 to Farnham Common, then turn west into Beeches Road. The main car park is straight ahead. Alternative parking is at the north-eastern corner, near a diamond-shaped earthwork known as 'the Moat'. **By train** The nearest train station is Burnham (National Rail Enquiries, 08457 484950).

By bus Bus no.70 from Beaconsfield, High Wycombe and Slough (0871 200 2233, www.traveline.org.uk). **On foot** From the information centre by the main car park, walking routes branch off the main footpaths, known as Halse Drive, Lord Mayor's Drive or Sir Henry Parks Drive (these are signposted). A circuit of the main routes takes one to two hours (but pick up a map from the information centre, or print one from the website); allow an afternoon for exploring the side paths. There is a short, fully accessible 'sensory trail' near the information centre. For wilder landscapes, park by the Moat, then cross Park Lane and follow paths into Dorney Wood or Egypt Wood. Dogs must be on a lead. **By bicycle** Cycling is permitted on tarmac routes only. **Map** Ordnance Survey Explorer 172, Chiltern Hills East; grid ref SU950851.

FURTHER REFERENCE

Burnham Beeches Office (01753 647358, www.cityoflondon.gov.uk/burnham). Toilets and refreshments are available at the information centre in the car park.

Ditchling Beacon

Sussex appeal.

From the vantage point of Ditchling Beacon, the undulating contours of what Rudyard Kipling called the 'blunt, bow-headed, whale-backed downs' stretch as far as the eye can see. To the west, the South Downs Way dips and climbs the chalk escarpment for some 50 miles, back to Hampshire; eastwards on the horizon lies the hazy blue-grey outline of the cliffs at the Seven Sisters, where the downs finally reach the sea.

The Victorians, like many modern-day visitors, preferred the drama of nearby Devil's Dyke, five miles along the ridge – a plunging, vertiginous gulf, carved out from the chalk strata as the Ice Age snowfields retreated. Day trippers flocked to peer into the abyss; in its tourist heyday at the end of the 19th century, there was even a cable car, perilously strung across the valley. But the Beacon, rising steeply above the villages and farmland of the Weald on one side, then sloping gently southwards down towards the sea, has its own quiet pleasures and oblique charms.

It is a landscape shaped by centuries of sheep grazing – the most profitable use for these bare, precipitous inclines, with their shallow, chalky soils. The constant grazing soon put paid to any saplings or taller plants that took root on the close-cropped slopes, letting shorter, less showy species thrive. As the naturalist and novelist WH Hudson observed in *Nature in Downland*, published in 1900: 'the luxury of long stems, the delight of waving in the wind, and the ambition to overtop their neighbours, would here be fatal.' Instead, as he notes, 'the turf is composed of small grasses and clovers mixed with a great variety of creeping herbs, some exceedingly small'. Seen at ground level – as you stretch out at full length on the soft, springy turf – the seemingly bare hillside is a miniature kingdom, teeming with life.

Richest of all are the unexpectedly sheltered, sunny banks and gullies that lie on the northern scarp slope of the hill, every bit as lulling as the bank on which Titania slept in *A Midsummer Night's Dream*, 'where the wild thyme blows/Where oxslips and the nodding violet grows'. Here, fragrant wild marjoram and thyme grow alongside delicate, lacy salad burnet leaves and tremulous harebells; the indomitable Hudson reports counting 64 harebells in a single square yard on Ditchling Beacon one late August afternoon. Rosette-shaped dwarf thistles stud the turf, and yellow bird's-foot trefoil, purple autumn gentian and the vivid blue unfurlings of round-headed rampion (the 'pride of Sussex') sprinkle the slopes with colour. The flowers, in turn, bring butterflies: common blues and painted ladies, rare silver-spotted skippers or the sudden, iridescent flash of a chalkhill blue.

Lilliputian treasures reward sharp eyes: a paper-thin snail shell, bleached white by the sun and ringed with ghostly striations, or a patch of eyebright, its clustered pink-tinged flowers resembling doll's-house lilies. Even the plants' names have their own peculiar charm: lady's bedstraw, fairy flax, quaking grass, hairy violet and squinancywort – traditionally used as a remedy against the quinsy (an inflammation of the tonsils).

With their gentle contours and wide-open vistas, these are benign, not brooding, hills. Ditchling Beacon's role has always been protective: an Iron Age hill fort – now a series of grassy hollows – once stood on its summit, and in 1588 the beacon that gives the hill its name was lit here, warning of the Spanish Armada's approach. The vast cloud shadows that occasionally chase across the hillside soon pass, and the smooth slopes are a world away from the tangled patches of ancient woodland below. The only sound is the whirr of crickets in the scrubland, or the high-pitched cry of a buzzard – a distant speck suspended overhead, scanning the open grassland for rabbits and voles.

During World War II, vast tracts of the downs were turned over to arable farming. As a result, swathes of farmland now sweep into the valleys near the reserves on the Beacon. Much of the terrain proved too steep for crops, though, and the upper reaches are a tangle of wild flowers and meadow grasses. In the ploughed lower fields, traditional farmland birds – small, dun-coloured buntings and fluting yellowhammers – scavenge for

The landscape at Ditchling has been shaped by centuries of sheep grazing.

grain. Peregrine falcons nest at the base of the hill in abandoned chalk quarries, which provided lime to fertilise the fields; in early summer, their grassy depths are dotted with tiny musk orchids and vivid pink pyramidal orchids.

Narrow, ancient bostalls (Anglo-Saxon for hill path) climb the slope from the tiny parishes down in the Weald; once used by villagers grazing their sheep, they have been engraved into the hillside by centuries of use. Running along the crest of the hill, the South Downs Way was used as a drovers' route to the great sheep fairs at Findon and Lewes. One of the dew ponds where the shepherds watered their flocks lies on a hillside to the west of the Beacon: a perfectly round, shallow dimple, lined with clay and guarded by twisted hawthorns. Further on are the 19th-century Clayton windmills, known as Jack and Jill, half-hidden behind a tangled copse.

Smaller, more capricious pathways weave around the flanks of Ditchling Beacon, lined with brambles, old man's beard and wayfaring trees. Their twists and turns yield unexpected delights, plunging you into rustling copses, then emerging into sun-dappled clearings, full of butterflies, or cutting through shoulder-high swathes of hemp agrimony and their sea of pink flowers. Others end as unexpectedly as they began, petering out in shadowy, overgrown spinneys of hawthorn and ash; long kept at bay by grazing, the woods are slowly advancing.

Most exhilarating of all, though, are the sudden steep ascents, on paths that are little more than a series of chalky footholds hewn into the sheer slope. And at the top? No café, no toilets, and certainly no cable car: just the spirit-lifting sweep of the Sussex Weald and the white ribbon of the South Downs Way, entering its homeward straight.

OTHER BEAUTY SPOTS

Those with an appetite for a climb and a taste for the unusual should walk from Ditchling Beacon to the Chattri Monument, near Patcham, dedicated to Indian soldiers of the First World War, who were hospitalised in Brighton after being wounded on the Western Front, and later died. Fifty-three Hindu soldiers were cremated on a ghat, built on the bare

Ditchling Beacon lies on the South Downs Way, a 100-mile footpath that runs between Winchester and Eastbourne.

hillside on the spot where the domed marble monument now stands. Set amid a gently sloping field of yellow rock roses, wild poppies and meadow grass, surrounded by faded remembrance wreaths, it's a strange but beautifully tranquil final resting place.

The cable car, funicular railway and funfair at Devil's Dyke are no more, but the sublime, sweeping views remain. A five-mile walk along the South Downs Way from Ditchling Beacon, it is popular with walkers, picnickers and hang-gliders. Stop for a half at the pub at the summit – an unlovely, squat construction – then admire the views across the weald below; 'perhaps the most grand & affecting natural landscape in the world – and consequently, a scene the most unfit for a picture,' according to John Constable.

East of Lewes, Malling Down (01273 492630, www.sussexwt.org.uk) is a sunny, steep stretch of chalk grassland, grazed by skittish sheep and famous for its wild flowers and butterflies. On sunny days, common blues, painted ladies and marbled whites cover the hillside – though the star is the brilliantly hued Adonis blue. Orchids also thrive here.

WHERE TO STAY & EAT

Set amid the half-timbered houses on Ditchling's narrow high street, the Bull (01273 843147, www.thebullditchling.com) has cask ales, sterling local lamb on the menu and four luxurious rooms, with rain showers, enormous beds and beautiful views. Across the road is the village deli, Chesterton's (01273 846638), which does a fine line in picnic provisions, and serves simple lunches in a sunny little walled garden.

If you'd rather sleep in the great outdoors, the campsite at Blackberry Wood in Streat (01273 890035, www.blackberrywood.com) is a delightfully small-scale operation, with 20 pitches set in leafy woodland clearings. Head to the Half Moon (01273 890253, www.halfmoonplumpton.com) in nearby Plumpton for log fires and stellar British food (warm pork pie with homemade chutney, wild rabbit stew). Another option is the Shepherd & Dog (01273 857382, www.shepherdanddogpub.co.uk) in Fulking – a 17th-century inn set at the foot of the downs, with low, beamed ceilings and a glorious beer garden. At Ditchling Beacon itself, there is often an ice-cream van in the car park during the summer.

Wild flowers flourish on Ditchling's sunny slopes.

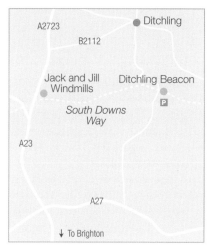

HOW TO GET THERE

Ditchling Beacon lies 3.5 miles north of Brighton in the South Downs. **By road** Follow the signs to Ditchling and Ditchling Beacon at the Holingbury junction of the A27, or turn off the B2116 at Ditchling Village, then take the Ditchling Beacon turning. There is a pay-and-display National Trust car park at the summit, or a small car park at the base of the hill, on Underhill Road.

By train Hassocks is the nearest station. **By bus** The 79 bus runs from Brighton Old Steine to the Beacon on Saturdays, Sundays and public holidays from April to Sept, then Sundays and bank holidays from October to March. For more information, call 01273 292480. **On foot** Ditchling Beacon is on the South Downs Way; for details, see www. nationaltrail.co.uk. Smaller footpaths also lead up to the Beacon from the villages in the weald. Note that the twisting, narrow road that runs between Ditchling Village and the Beacon is unsafe for pedestrians. **By bicycle** Cyclists can follow the South Downs Way – or tackle Beacon Road, up from Ditchling Village, but be warned: the traffic is dangerous, and the hill steep. **Map** Ordnance Survey Explorer 122, Brighton & Hove; grid ref TQ331130.

FURTHER REFERENCE

Sussex Wildlife Trust (01273 492630, www.sussexwt.org.uk). Visit South Downs (01243 558700, www. visitsouthdowns.com).

Hickling Broad

Give peace a chance.

'**V**ery flat – Norfolk.' So wrote Noël Coward in *Private Lives*. He could have added 'incredibly still'. The county's marshy topography has stifled development, and consequently things happen slowly here. You can hear it in the drawn-out vowels of the Norfolk accent and the placid, thoughtful speech of the locals; you can see it in the way people linger for hours when they've only popped in for a minute. But the county is at its most splendidly languid and lazy in the Norfolk Broads.

This sprawling network of seven rivers flows from Norwich, winding 20 miles east to the coast, although their myriad tributaries twist and turn for 125 miles. The Broads are also studded with 63 inland lakes, most less than 13 feet deep, all a long way from civilisation. And they are fringed with reeds, marsh and woodlands. Walking gingerly through the wetlands, sitting on a boat travelling at four miles per hour or listening to rivers lap against the banks, one feels the world slow right down, as the water, woods and sky create poetry in (slow) motion. Man-made sights, such as medieval bridges, windmills and beautifully proportioned flint churches are, for once, in harmony with the landscape.

The otherworldliness of the Broads is down to a combination of history and nature. Until the 1960s, they were thought to be natural features created by the sea's reclamation of land. But they are, in fact, ancient flooded pits – some just a few feet across, others two or three miles wide – created by the excavation of peat for fuel, first by the Romans, then by medieval monasteries. But when sea levels rose in the 15th century, the pits flooded. Channels linking them were dug out by fisherman and thatchers, who moulded 117 square miles of wetland into one of England's 'natural' wonders.

They unwittingly created one of England's great travel destinations. Each year, hundreds of thousands of people explore the Broads. They are drawn by the ease of

travel (there are no locks, and the rivers are tranquil), by the wildlife (more than 300 species of bird) and by that preternatural quiet and slow pace. There are exceptions – Wroxham, the self-proclaimed Norfolk Broads capital, is bustling – but there is one place that guarantees peace, even on a summer Sunday. On Hickling Broad, a few miles north of cheesy, cheery Great Yarmouth, you feel worlds away – it's easy to imagine yourself travelling up Vietnam's Nung river in a Little Englander remake of *Apocalypse Now*.

The departure point for this watery world is Potter Heigham, a charming and quiet village. The peaceful air is down to the Old Bridge, a hump-backed arch over the River Thurne; it's so small, only day boats can squeeze underneath. This keeps the stretch of water between here and Hickling empty, as do the swirling currents under the bridge.

Once through, however, the intrepid dayboater is rewarded with some lovely bankside sights: pretty fretworked wooden cottages or larger *Little House on the Prairie*-style dwellings topped with reed thatch and sedge trimmed from the Broads. With all the white picket fences and quaint wooden railings, you half expect to see Laura Ingalls waving gaily. Some of the houses feel very Middle England, with waterside gardens featuring plastic furniture and Venus de Milo copies, but civilisation quickly gives way to raw unspoiled beauty. Soon enough your only companions on the river are ducks, geese and swans. The sultry fen banks of reed and sedge are backed by wet woodland of alder and willow; behind this is dry woodland dominated by gnarled oaks.

The wildlife is similarly diverse and profuse. Even if you don't know a tit from a common tern, you'll be bowled over by the sheer variety of butterflies, dragonflies the size of toy remote-controlled copters, and birds, birds, birds – kingfishers, kestrel, tits, warblers and bittern all call Hickling home. The place names within Hickling are just as lovely as the birds themselves – Sound Plantation, say, or Whispering Reeds. Many of them have little moorings at which you can stop to listen and look. This is advisable: stopping the motorboat enables the silence, and the creatures, to surround you.

The rustling reeds, big skies and still waters are a recipe for relaxation.

At most small moorings, you won't be able to venture more than a few feet into the surrounding marshland. But traversing Hickling Broad via the marker channels will bring you to the ethereal National Nature Reserve, where you can penetrate the surrounding wetland via meandering trails and boardwalks. Here, one can hear the booming of the rare bittern in the Hundred Acre Reedbed, see the swallowtail butterfly fluttering among the milk parsley or touch delicate plants such as yellow flag iris and cotton grass. Spotting otters, wading birds and lizards is a Hickling sport – about as energetic as it gets around here. To fully soak up the Broads at their wettest and wildest, take the two-hour boat trip through the backwaters of Hickling (not navigable any other way). Then climb the tree tower, a 60-foot platform in the nature reserve, to take in the lie of this watery land. Up there, you'll fully appreciate how very flat – and still – Norfolk really is.

OTHER BEAUTY SPOTS

Horsey Mere, a windswept broad, is a vast wetland fringed by coastal dunes. The paths afford classic Broads views of rustling reeds, marshes and the birds that frequent them. There's a traditional 1911 windpump, owned by the National Trust, at Horsey Staithe; it was once used to drain the land for farming. A path through the open fields and woodland leads to Horsey beach, where colonies of grey seals often frolic.

From Norwich, the Wherry Line railway (0344 800 8003, www.wherrylines.org.uk) follows the rivers Wensum, Waveney and Yare to the marshland around Berney Arms Mill (01493 857900, www.english-heritage.org.uk). At 70 feet, this Victorian windmill is the tallest in Norfolk, but it is just as well-known for its bird life (the land here is an RSPB reserve). In winter, the marshes are blanketed by thousands of ducks, geese and swans; in spring, this is a haven for lapwing and redshank.

To sample another particularly pretty stretch of the Broads, take a day boat from Wroxham to Ranworth, cruising down the River Bure. On the way, Hoveton Great Broad has a nature trail that, on a hot day, has a whiff of the swampy Louisiana bayou about it. Ranworth itself is one of the prettiest Broads, with a boardwalk snaking through another wetland nature reserve. In Ranworth village, climb the tower of the 14th-century Ranworth Church, aka 'the cathedral of the Broads', for a sweeping view.

WHERE TO STAY & EAT

This part of Norfolk is a long way from the foodie mecca of the north Norfolk coast, but the riverside pubs usually serve hearty, home-cooked fare. The Nelson Head in Horsey (01493 393378, www.nelsonheadhorsey.co.uk) is a rustic pub that does a good steak and ale pie. At Horning, the Staithe n Willow (01692 630915) restaurant uses local produce, meat from Horning butcher and fresh seafood (Cromer crabs are a highlight), all served in a tea-room-style setting.

For accommodation, neither the Swan Inn at Horning (01692 630316) nor the Sutton Staithe Hotel (01692 580244, www.suttonstaithehotel.co.uk) are particularly stylish, but both overlook the river. For grander surroundings, Norfolk Mead (01603 737531, www. norfolkmead.co.uk) is a Georgian manor house on eight acres of riverside grounds. Some

rooms have four-poster beds and there's an outdoor pool. The elegant restaurant specialises in fresh and local: crabs, lobster, special breeds of meat and organic produce. Broad House (01603 783567, www.broadhousehotel.co.uk), a boutique country-house hotel, has period bedrooms, swish bathrooms and a rich colour scheme. The restaurant serves Modern British dishes: ham hock terrine with pea mousse and apple chutney, say, or local partridge with fondant potato. For true river holidays, a two-berth cruiser starts at £409 for a week with Norfolk Broads Direct (01692 670711, www.broads.co.uk).

Nearby Ranworth Broad is similarly soothing, with a boardwalk that snakes through dense greenery.

HOW TO GET THERE

Hickling Broad is in the the Norfolk Broads north-east of Norwich. **By road** From Norwich, take the A1151 past Wroxham, then take the A149 heading south past Stalham. You can either carry on to Potter Heigham and hire a boat, or turn east off A149 towards Catfield Common. From Hickling village, follow the brown duck tourist signs. **By train** From Norwich, the Bittern Line (www.bitternline.com) runs north through Wroxham, and the Wherry Lines (0344 800 8003, www.wherrylines.org.uk) go east to Great Yarmouth. **By bus** There is no service to Hickling but the no.54 offers a Mon-Sat service from Norwich (Castle Meadow, Stand B) to Broads villages Hoveton, Horning, Ludham and Stalham (0871 200 2233, www.travelineeast anglia.org.uk). The Acle area Flexibus (01493 752223) also serves many Broads villages. **By bicycle** The Broads by Bike map and booklet has details of nine circular routes, from 10 to 25 miles. Pick them up at a tourist office, or call 01603 610734. **On foot** The Weavers Way path runs close to the southern half of Hickling Broad. Hickling Nature Reserve (01692 598276) has boardwalk nature trails and lookout points, as does the NWT Broads Wildlife Centre (01603 625540, www.norfolkwildlifetrust.org.uk) in Ranworth. See also www.broads-authority.gov.uk. **By boat** Norfolk Broads Direct (01692 670711, www.broads.co.uk), in Potter Heigham and Wroxham, has everything from day boats to luxury cruisers. **Map** Ordnance Survey Explorer OL40, The Broads; grid ref TG415216.

FURTHER REFERENCE

Hickling Broads National Nature Reserve (01692 598276, www.norfolkwildlifetrust.org.uk). There are tourist information centres in Hoveton/Wroxham (01603 782281), as well as How Hill (01692 678763), Ludham (01692 678763), Potter Heigham (0692 677016), Ranworth (01603 270453) and Whitlingham (01603 617332). For all, see www.broadsauthority.gov.uk/visiting.html. See also www.visitnorfolk.co.uk.

The Wash

Expand your horizons.

The horizon stretches out into infinity: a muted palette of muddy marshland, beige sand dunes and khaki green grass. The slate grey water can barely muster enough vigour to lap against the sea wall. Above, the huge pale skies are speckled with thousands of wheeling grey knots, their mournful cry backed by the lonely rustle of reeds and whisper of wind. In the distance, it's hard to know where the sea ends and the land begins, such a blur is the stony-coloured water and flat brown horizon. The scene is neither charming nor chocolate box, yet in its emptiness lies a dramatic grandeur. Welcome to the Wash Estuary, Britain's unsung and understated beauty, where moody skies and flat horizons are, in their own way, as mesmerising as snow-capped mountains, dazzling beaches or rugged cliffs.

A giant groove cut into the coast of East Anglia, between the North Sea and the vulnerable flat farmlands of the Fens, the Wash is an intriguing place. Its vast networks of sand dunes and salt marshes, which stretch across Norfolk and Lincolnshire, are both a natural and a man-made border with the sea. But in this nebulous landscape, borders are elusive. As the tide retreats, it reveals land that is neither seabed nor mainland, a dichotomy that lends the Wash – and its 65,000 acres of tidal mudflats and 10,000 acres of salt marsh – its fluid character.

Land and sea tend to blur together in the wide open spaces of the Wash, pictured here at Gibraltar Point.

Though quiet these days, the farmlands of the Wash would once have bustled. A beneficiary of the Hanseatic League, a medieval trade alliance across northern Europe, Lincolnshire grew rich on wool, and prosperous merchants funded large local churches – notice the distinctive spires in Long Sutton and Boston. Mighty windmills were used to power drainage pumps for crop fields. The windmills and low-lying fields instantly recall the Netherlands: no wonder the region is nicknamed 'Little Holland'. The town of Spalding even holds an annual tulip parade in May, when thousands of acres are bathed in colour.

While not always so dramatic, the never-ending fieldscapes are the area's big draw. The sky is an epic tableau, to which novelist Charles Kingsley found his eyes inexorably drawn: 'Overhead the arch of heaven spread more ample than elsewhere, as over the open sea; and that vastness gave, and still gives, such cloudlands, such sunrises, such sunsets, as can be seen nowhere else within these isles.' These infinite horizons seem to have inspired a cluster of home-grown explorers. The Pilgrim Fathers first attempted to set sail from Boston in 1607; Sir John Franklin, of Spilsby, perished trying to navigate the Northwest Passage of America; King's Lynn-born George Vancouver was more successful when launching for Canada. John Smith, a principal settler of Jamestown, Virginia (best remembered for his meetings with Pocahontas), came from Willoughby-by-Alford, while Horatio, Lord Nelson, was born just across the border in Norfolk.

Not that explorers own all the imaginative rights to the Wash. Poet laureate Alfred, Lord Tennyson grew up nearby and wanderlust manifested itself in his consciousness too. He could have been gazing at the Wash when he wrote:

All experience is an arch wherethro'/gleams that untravelled world whose margin fades/for ever and for ever when I move. …/'Tis not too late to seek a newer world.

The solitary splendour of the Wash is showcased on the 12-mile Sir Peter Scott Walk, which starts at the East Lighthouse, near Sutton Bridge. The great conservationist once

lived here, breeding geese and painting wildlife. Scott founded the Wildfowl and Wetlands Trust, and co-founded the World Wildlife Fund, designing their famous panda logo. The walk named after him is unnervingly featureless: the bleak loneliness of the sea wall broken up only by the occasional grazing cow. But the isolation can be liberating and inspirational, too. James Wentworth Day, author of *The Modern Fowler* (1934), always felt a rush of excitement beneath the open skies: 'I think that if one were to live in this wide and open country of great fields and great seascapes, where the horizons are wide as the sea itself… and the geese last saw land beneath the Midnight Sun, one might walk like a hero, live like a fighting cock, and die at a hundred.'

The horizons are still as vast as they were in Wentworth Day's epoch, but the Peter Scott walk lets you take in the desolate Wash in one long, sweeping glance. In the

distance to the north-east, you can see the Hunstanton lighthouse, gateway to the Wash from the Norfolk side. In the opposite direction, to the north-west, lies Skegness: with its flashing arcade games and donkey rides, it is a brash anomaly in these parts.

The Wash is all about natural thrills. The estuary forms part of the East Atlantic Flyway from Arctic Greenland and Siberia to Africa, an avian motorway. At high tide, flocks of up to 120,000 knots may pass overhead, churning up the air with their flapping. Barn owls like the drainage dykes in the Fens farmland. They hunt water vole, which flourish around the Wash, as does the brown hare, which makes its warrens in flat land. Redshank feed in such grazed areas, while in the longer grass, seed-eating birds like skylarks and pippets provide an incongruously cheerful soundtrack to the desolate landscape. Offshore, inquisitive seals pop their heads above the water, gathering to breed up the coast at Donna Nook in late autumn and winter.

Birds outnumber humans in the stark Wash, and nowhere is this more true than at Gibraltar Point, a Lincolnshire nature reserve with an almost magical aura of tranquillity. A short drive from the kiss-me-quick chaos of Skegness, but worlds away in feel, the reserve is sheer escapism, courtesy of the Royal Society for the Protection of Birds (RSPB). Here, clover-fragranced paths criss-cross a network of dunes and scrub; smaller tracks lead off to bird hides, where you can watch unsuspecting avians pick through the sea purslane along meandering creeks, or take cover amid bushy sea buckthorn. Deviate from the paths and you'll find yourself among bright yellow fields of flowers, or small wooded copses. It's a patchwork of chalky sand dunes, salt marsh and freshwater marsh and field, all blending hazily into one – the Wash in a nutshell.

Gibraltar Point National Nature Reserve combines marshy wetlands, delicate flora and fauna and vast coastal horizons.

OTHER BEAUTY SPOTS

The RSPB (01205 724678, www.rspb.org.uk) has three reserves along this stretch of coast. Frampton Marsh is notable for its scrapes – shallow, water-filled dips, beloved of breeding lapwing. Waders such as avocet and redshank feed off the plentiful invertebrates in the mudflats – lugworms, ragworms, snails, cockles and mussels. Birds of prey abound, too: peregrine falcons in winter, marsh harriers in summer, and more kestrels than anywhere in the country.

Freiston Shore was created from major land reclamation in the 1970s and '80s, when a flood defence was deliberately breached to create a new saltmarsh. Avocets and redshank stalk the samphire, and brent geese abound in winter, when the sound of twites fills the air. Snettisham, meanwhile, with its inter-tidal mudflats and brackish gravel pits, hosts tens of thousands of birds, especially knots. In autumn, migratory birds swell the numbers – up to 55,000 pink-footed geese from Greenland and Iceland descend.

The Wash is also graced by the presence of Sandringham, the stunning royal estate (01553 612908, www.sandringhamestate.co.uk). Attached are 600 acres of country park, with a pine, oak and birch forest, which are free and open all year.

The Peter Scott Walk in Norfolk captures the moody glory of the Wash.

WHERE TO STAY & EAT

Congham Hall (01485 600250, www.conghamhallhotel.co.uk), the grandest local hotel, is a peaceful Georgian country manor in Grimston, Norfolk, with a bucolic herb garden, acres of paddocks and a croquet lawn. Their Orangery restaurant is perhaps the best (formal) dining option in the area.

Smart Cley Hall in Spalding (01775 725157, www.cleyhallhotelspalding.co.uk), a Georgian Grade-II listed hotel, also offers formal and slightly-less-formal dining options.

Overlooking the Ouse in King's Lynn, the 18th-century Bank House Hotel (01553 660492, www.thebankhouse.co.uk) has 11 individually decorated rooms with very comfortable beds, and a restaurant that does hearty dishes well: roast cod with crushed new potatoes and cherry tomatoes went down a treat.

Bateman's Brewery (01754 880317, www.bateman.co.uk), in Wainfleet All Saints, Lincolnshire, is an old family brewery in a riverside windmill. Drink the real ale at the visitor centre, or sample the suds in a local pub, like the King's Head in Freiston (01205 760368). On the other side of the waters, try the Hare Arms in Stow Bardolph (01366 382229, www.theharearms.co.uk), which has a peacock garden and excellent pub food.

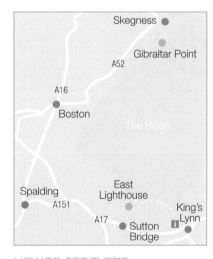

HOW TO GET THERE

The Wash Estuary lies on the East Anglia coast between Norfolk and Lincolnshire. The boundaries are Old Hunstanton in Norfolk in the east and Skegness in Lincolnshire to the north-west. King's Lynn is a good base: take the A17 north and explore the bay on the small roads leading off it. Boston is closer to Gibraltar Point. A car is almost essential. **By car**
The A17 between King's Lynn and Boston is the major road in the south; in the north, the A52 between Skegness and Boston. **By train** King's Lynn, or Skegness for Gibraltar Point (National Rail Enquiries, 08457 484950). **By bus** The Norfolk Green Bus no.505 (01553 776980, www.norfolkgreen.co.uk) from King's Lynn to Sutton Bridge. Walk or take a taxi from here (01406 364135, £8) to East Lighthouse. **On foot** The Sir Peter Scott Walk is a 12-mile walk from East Lighthouse on the east side of the River Nene to West Lynn Ferry (07974 260639), which crosses to King's Lynn. **Map Ordnance Survey** Explorer 249/250/261/274, Spalding & Holbeach/Norfolk Coast, West/Boston/Skegness, Alford & Spilsby; grid ref TF520425.

FURTHER REFERENCE

King's Lynn Tourist Information Centre (01553 763044, www.visitnorfolk.co.uk). See also www.lincolnshirewildlifetrust.org.uk; www.visitlincolnshire.com.

Wye Valley

Picture perfect.

In nature as in name, the Wye Valley is defined by its river, a 185-mile ribbon of water that begins in the Welsh mountains and ends in the Severn Estuary near Chepstow. Rivers, like men, play many parts, and the Wye is at once presiding genius and guiding thread; sometimes English, sometimes Welsh, sometimes a liquid boundary between the two once warring sides. In its clean currents swim some of the best salmon in the British Isles, and in the clean air above and around are some of the loveliest prospects of woodland, meadows and steep-sided rock to be seen anywhere.

The most scenic part of the valley is the river's downstream third, and the surrounding territory that makes up one of Britain's 45 Areas of Outstanding Natural Beauty. Like the course of any river, the valley of the Wye has been created by a combination of water work and geological circumstance – in this case, a motley of limestones and sand-stones that informs the land's startling swings of mood. At the AONB's northern end, the river meanders in lazy loops across a large floodplain between the range of hills known as the Woolhope Dome and, 12 miles to the south, Ross-on-Wye; but then, at Goodrich, it enters the famous Wye Gorge that runs, with occasional interruptions, all the way to the Severn, passing an almost unbroken line of ancient woodland (Wordsworth dubbed the Wye a 'wanderer through the woods') as it goes.

The gorge is the Lower Wye's focal point and, for many people, its quintessence. This is where you'll find its most spectacular stretches of scenery. The river zigzags between steep-sided hills and rugged cliffs, overhung at its edges by mature broadleaf trees and, for long stretches, shunning all signs of human habitation. In the 19th century, the Wye carried commercial cargo, but today the traffic is mostly canoes; hire one at the right time of an out-of-season day, and you can paddle round a bend and find yourself alone on the water, gliding downstream through what feels like a lost world.

Nowhere is the scenery more impressive than at Symonds Yat, four miles upstream of Monmouth; indeed, the panorama from Symonds Yat Rock, high above the river, is one of the most photographed and painted vistas in England. On the left, the dense canopy of deciduous trees on Huntsham Hill rolls all the way down to the river, which snakes elegantly to its vanishing point past wide meadows on the other bank. It's a beautiful sight in any season, and especially in autumn, when Coppet Hill in the middle distance turns a deep, ruddy bronze as ferns dry out on its flank. In the cliffs behind the great vantage point is a colony of peregrine falcons, visible through coin-operated telescopes.

Coppet Hill goes out in a blaze of glory in autumn.

Once out of sight, the river doubles sharply back and enters one of the most narrow, high-sided sections of the gorge, a segment that has loud rapids, the Biblins campsite and the Seven Sisters, monumental knuckles of limestone that protrude above the trees. A couple of miles, and another U-turn further on, and the wilderness feeling vanishes as the river is shadowed by the A466 dual carriageway; the next impression of remoteness doesn't come until the river has passed Tintern, over ten miles to the south.

Even where the mark of humankind is clear, however, there's much to please the eye. The abundance, rich variety and sheer character of the trees stand out in nearly any view of the district – much of which, away from the rocky showpieces of the gorge, is placidly rolling farmland. Noble oaks, beeches, maples, yews and chestnuts are legion; and, on a smaller scale but no less beguiling, the local flora is marvellously diverse, from the common types like bluebells, red campion and oxeye daisies, and the rare plants such as dwarf sedge and the appropriately named ghost orchid. The hedges abound with different microspecies of bramble, which are so outwardly similar that distinguishing between them is best done with the tongue, in August, when the bland fruit of one hangs just yards from the sensational blackberries of another.

Birds take both kinds, of course – although the most glamorous flyers in the Wye Valley, the frequently seen kingfishers and buzzards, and the much rarer peregrines, are not partial to fruit. Such star turns are just a tiny proportion of an enormous miscellany of birds – migrant and resident – including familiar farmland types, ravens and, at the estuary where the river empties, a wealth of waders. The gorge is noted for its large numbers of horseshoe bats; and on the ground, badgers are common, deer are elusive but by no means invisible, and otters and polecats, once wiped out here, have recently been making a comeback.

With so much natural beauty, good fishing, good air, and much to interest geologists, lepidopterists, botanists and naturalists, it's hardly surprising that the Wye Valley has long attracted tourists. In fact, the area has been described as Britain's first tourist destination, a state of affairs that began when a clergyman called William Gilpin was taken down the river from Ross in 1770, and wrote a favourable book about what he saw. The book launched the 'Wye Tour', patriotically touted as a match for anything the Continent had to offer, and by the mid 19th century, people were coming in their thousands. Painters, including Turner, fuelled the vogue by recording what became classic Wye scenes, notably the Cistercian abbey at Tintern, one of the finest monastic ruins in the British Isles. And the discovery of significant Palaeolithic human and animal remains in King Arthur's Cave near Symonds Yat aroused scholarly attention.

Palaeolithic human remains were found inside King Arthur's Cave.

Yet, astonishingly, the Wye Valley in the 21st century is one of Britain's least- renowned beauty spots. Wordsworth's 'Lines Written above Tintern Abbey', the much-anthologised poem, keeps that ruin fresh in literary minds, and Symonds Yat is busy in summer; but elsewhere, crowds are conspicuous by their absence. And long may that situation continue, as the few people who do visit can easily find footpaths, hillsides and woods that give them the feeling of having the countryside to themselves. Indeed, out of season, even the star attractions are quiet – and Tintern Abbey rising above the mist on an early spring morning, romantic, holy and deserted, is something one remembers for itself, not for the yammer and bustle that often mar celebrated sites in other parts of the country.

OTHER BEAUTY SPOTS

A vantage point high on the steep banks of Capler Wood, a mile south of Fownhope on the eastern bank of the Wye, affords superb views over the mild pastures below. From here, a footpath leads further up to Capler Camp, an old Iron Age fort whose outline is

still clearly visible. It's a romantic spot and very little visited, and the view is nothing short of idyllic. The subterranean counterparts to such overland beauty are Clearwell Caves (www.clearwellcaves.com), a network of nine caverns just outside Coleford. The atmospheric caves were formed naturally, then enlarged by the mining of iron ore over thousands of years; guided tours of deeper chambers can be arranged.

WHERE TO STAY & EAT

Although the historic town of Monmouth is just outside the AONB, it stands next to the river and makes a good base from which to explore the whole of the Lower Wye. Steppes Farm (01600 775424, www.steppesfarmcottages.co.uk), in undulating countryside three miles north-west of the town centre, has half a dozen pretty stone cottages that still show their 17th-century agricultural origins, but also have a high level of modern comfort. Its Stone Mill restaurant serves contemporary cuisine in a 16th-century barn.

At Chepstow, the Marriott St Pierre Hotel and Country Club (01291 625261, www.marriott.co.uk) occupies an even older building: a 14th-century manor with castellated gate house and extensive parkland.

The sublime landscapes are complemented by placid rolling farmland, such as these cornfields near Capler Camp.

For food, few establishments in the AONB can match the Bridge (01989 562655, www.bridge-house-hotel.com) in Wilton, just outside Ross-on-Wye, winner of the Flavours of Herefordshire best restaurant award four years running: its gourmet fare, such as a fine tart of leeks and shallots served with a garlic velouté, is made with impeccable local ingredients. A 'restaurant with rooms', the Bridge also has accommodation. So does the smart Crown (01600 860254, www.crownatwhitebrook.co.uk), which is halfway between Monmouth and Tintern in Whitebrook, and has the only Michelin star in Wales. Its eight bedrooms, done in tasteful neutral tones, are similarly upmarket.

HOW TO GET THERE

The Wye Valley AONB is a north–south strip roughly 30 miles long and between four and eight miles wide. Its northern border is halfway between Hereford and Ledbury, its southernmost point at Chepstow. **By road** The M48 and M50 are the nearest motorways; the A466 runs through Tintern and the heart of the southern half of the Area of Natural Beauty, and the A40 cuts diagonally across the northern half, passing near Symonds Yat and Ross-on-Wye. **By train** Chepstow and Hereford are the nearest stations (National Rail Enquiries, 08457 484950). **By bus** National Express runs regular services to Hereford and Ross-on-Wye; fairly frequent local services are operated by Stagecoach (www.stagecoach.com) between the main towns and many villages. **On foot** Signposted public footpaths criss-cross the Area of Natural Beauty; the most scenic is the Wye Valley Walk (www.wyevalleywalk.org). Footpath maps and suggested rambling routes are available from tourist offices (*see below*). **By bicycle** The hilly terrain of the Wye Valley makes for a tough ride, but the rewards are rich. An easy and scenic stretch runs from Goodrich, just south of Ross-on-Wye, along the river to Symonds Yat. Bikes and gear can be hired in Ross at Revolutions (48 Broad Street, 01989 562639). **By boat** Canoes can be hired at Symonds Yat (01600 891069, www.canoehire.com); river cruises operate in summer and autumn from two nearby moorings (Kingfisher Cruises, 01600 891063; Wye Valley Cruises, 07815 001698). **Map** Ordnance Survey Explorer OL14, Wye Valley & Forest of Dean; grid ref SO581187.

FURTHER REFERENCE

The main tourist offices are at Chepstow (01291 623772), Monmouth (01600 713899) and Ross-on-Wye (01989 562768); for all, see www.visitwyevalley.com. See also www.southernwales.com and www.visitherefordshire.co.uk.

Vale of Evesham

Blooming marvellous.

The Vale of Evesham may sound familiar, but it's curiously hard to place. It's in Worcestershire, but doesn't include Worcester; it's not officially the Cotswolds, though one of the Cotswolds' most popular villages, Broadway, lies in the Vale; it's not Stratford-upon-Avon, though Shakespeare's Avon is its river; and it's not the Malverns, though Elgar was inspired by the views of it. It's also the middle of Middle England, yet a relatively hidden corner of a very countrified countryside. And yet this unsung valley has two claims to fame: it's the fabled setting of *The Archers*, BBC's long-running radio soap, and it's the fruit basket of England. Set in the fertile flood plain of the River Avon, and sheltered by hills on three sides, this rural bowl has a mild microclimate that has yielded a patchwork of orchards, market gardens, dairy and arable farmland. Threaded with narrow lanes, the peaceful landscape offers glimpses of the distant blue hills through gaps in the hedgerows. Calm and unspectacular most of the year, the Vale turns on the charm every spring, when its apple, plum and pear trees paint a lovely picture.

From late March to early May, the florid spectacle brings increased traffic to this rural idyll. The Blossom Trail, a waymarked route showcasing the best of the blooms, lures scenery-chasing cyclists, day-tripping motorists and camera-snapping coach tours. The tours may not match the Japanese tradition of *hanami* – full-on saké-drinking festivals that celebrate that country's legendary cherry blossoms – but they're not far removed in spirit. The Japanese shindigs, for instance, are less about the fecundity of nature than about their concept of '*mono no aware*' – a sensitivity to life's passing. Similarly, in the

Vale of Evesham, the fruit blossoms become more poignant every year: the orchards are fast disappearing as they are uprooted to make way for more profitable crops. If this continues, what a loss it will be. With their frothy clusters of palest pink and white flowers nodding delicately in the breeze, rank after rank of them foaming along hillsides, they temporarily transform this patch of green and pleasant Englishness into a palette of pastels, Britain's low-key answer to springtime in Tokyo.

The Blossom Trail begins in Pershore, a doughty market town surrounded by orchards; in April, its approach roads are lined with startling pink cherry blossoms. Pershore is also the place to start an *Archers* pilgrimage: it may well be the inspiration for Borchester, the fictional market town. It's certainly got a storybook feel: set on the River Avon, it has an impressive abbey church, a handsome Georgian high street and a proper town square. On the edge of town, the famous horticultural college – celebrity alumni include Monty Don and Alan Titchmarsh – still nurtures green-fingered students. Meanwhile, the nearby village of Inkberrow is the model for *The Archers'* main setting, Ambridge. Series creator Godfrey Baseley hailed from these parts and real events from the village once featured in the soap. Coachloads of fans now descend, hoping to meet Eddie Grundy in his cups at the Bull pub, or Lynda Snell arranging flowers in the church.

The Vale of Evesham is renowned for its blossom trail, a florid spectacle that usually lasts from late March until early May.

The heart of the Vale is the market garden town of Evesham. It was severely flooded in 1999 and again in 2007, but has bounced back. With its riverside events (a busy regatta and an angling competition in August), its medieval history (the rebellion of Simon de Montfort, who was calling for a directly elected parliament, came to a bloody end here in the 13th century), and the remains of the third-largest abbey in England, Evesham is almost as lovely as it sounds, though the locals pronounce it 'Asum'. The town museum provides insight into the fruits of the Vale's earth. The rich potash soil – combined with the nourishing waters of the Avon, used for irrigation – has always been conducive to a bumper crop (the Domesday Book, published in 1086, recorded 38 vineyards in the Vale). It's a vegetable patch too: everything from onions to leeks, spinach to broccoli flourishes here. The asparagus fields have a distinctive ridge and furrow that is easy to discern, but if you need help there are spring Asparagus Tours (see p131).

Broadway, a quaint and handsome village, is the most touristy destination on the Blossom Trail, thanks to its association with the Cotswolds: it lies at the foot of the famous hills, and its buildings are made of honey-coloured Cotswold stone. In spring, there are irresistible views of the town from Broadway Tower, once home to William Morris;

The Vale of Evesham is also known as the fruit basket of England, owing to its abundance of orchards.

Broadway's Gordon Russell Museum honours the local craftsman who embraced the teachings of the Victorian Arts and Crafts guru.

The blossom trail peaks north of Evesham, near a clutch of villages called the Lenches. Set amid low, rolling hills, the hamlets of Church Lench, Sheriffs Lench and Abbott's Lench burst with colour in April. Things get off to a subtle start: the white plum and damson trees bloom first, in late March, along with the white blossoms of the blackthorn. The bright pink cherry trees come hard on their heels; two weeks later, the delicate pink-and-white apple blossoms dapple the horizon. From a distance, the orchards look as though there's been a controlled riot by pointillist painters. Postcard vantage points are provided by the twee Evesham Vale Light Railway, a tiny tourist train that chugs over hills and through orchards.

Harder-earned vistas can be found from the summit of Bredon Hill, a lonely mound celebrated in sad verses by AE Housman. It's a fair hike to the top, but it leaves a lasting impression. Housman wasn't the only poet to wax lyrical about the area. Michael Drayton, the Elizabethan poet, swooned about Bredon in his epic poem 'Poly-Olbion', referring to its 'lofty hills', 'humble valleys' and 'high grace' and gushing about its 'delicious sweets'. Centuries on, those lofty hills and humble valleys are still worthy of poetry, especially during spring, when the blossoms work their magic.

OTHER BEAUTY SPOTS

The Malvern Hills, west of the Vale of Evesham, afford panoramic views of Hereford, Worcestershire and Gloucestershire. British Camp, an Iron Age hill fort above Eastnor Castle, overlooks the Vale, and its majestic setting inspired Elgar's music. To the south-west are the green and golden glories of the Cotswold hills.

Madresfield Court, due west of Evesham, is the extraordinary Elizabethan mansion that is thought to have inspired Evelyn Waugh's *Brideshead Revisited* (01905 830680, www.elmley.org.uk, by appointment only).

Snowshill Manor (01386 852 410, www.nationaltrust.org.uk) (pronounced 'snozzle'), south of Broadway, is a medieval Cotswold Manor house with an Arts and Craft Garden, set in gorgeous, rolling green countryside. Once home to Charles Paget Wade, an eccentric Edwardian collector, it's stuffed full of crafts, design and artefacts from around the globe. The pond-filled gardens have views over the Vale of Evesham.

Pershore Abbey dates from 1100; the town of Pershore is said to be the inspiration for Borchester, the market town in *The Archers*.

WHERE TO STAY & EAT

The high-end option is Broadway's 16th-century Lygon Arms (01386 852255, www. barcelo-hotels.co.uk), with its liveried footmen, elegant restaurant and classically styled indoor pool. The period feel is enhanced by the flagstone floors and beamed ceilings. The Evesham Hotel (01386 765566, www.zen37209.zen.co.uk) is the most eccentric choice: it has teddy-bear keyrings, themed rooms (safari, Egyptian, nautical) and an indoor pool that is guarded by a life-sized gorilla; the restaurant is as child-friendly as the hotel.

In Pershore, the Angel Inn Hotel (01386 552 046, www.angelpershore.co.uk) is an old coaching inn with tastefully refurbished bedrooms; its restaurant does a well-rounded medley of steaks, roasts, pizza and pasta.

Lower End House (01386 751600, www.lowerendhouse.co.uk) in Eckington is a chic and luxurious B&B in an old farmhouse. Nearby, the Eckington Manor Cookery School (01386 751600, www.eckingtonmanorcookeryschool.co.uk) runs acclaimed courses.

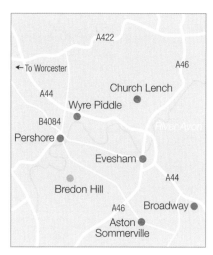

HOW TO GET THERE

The Vale of Evesham is in Worcestershire, centred around the town of Evesham.
By car The M5 skirts the west of the Vale (take Junction 7 for Pershore), about 30 minutes south of Birmingham. Evesham is 30 minutes north of Cheltenham (M40/A40). **By road** The Blossom Trail follows a rough figure of eight round Pershore and Evesham, following the B4084 northwest out of Pershore, then the A44 southeast through Wyre Piddle, with a detour northwards round the Lenches, to Evesham and then onward on the A44 southeast to Broadway. It then heads back northwest to Pershore via Aston Somerville, crossing the A46 at Hinton Cross and joining the B4084 again via Haselor. Blossom trail maps from tourist information. **By train** Pershore and Evesham are the nearest stations (National Rail Enquiries, 08457 484950). **By bus** There are coach tours of the Blossom Trail on Wednesdays in April (01386 792206, www.dudleys-coaches.co.uk; Wychavon District Council at 01386 565373). **On foot** There is a three-mile walk from All Saints in Church Lench, through Atch Lench past orchards. There is a 4.5-mile walk from the recreation ground in Fladbury past apple and pear orchards. There is a six-mile walk from Tiddesley Wood Nature Reserve near Pershore. Call 01386 565373 for details. **By bicycle** The blossom trail is also a bike route, signposted from Evesham railway station. **Map** Ordnance Survey Explorer 205, Stratford-upon-Avon & Evesham; grid ref SP027440.

FURTHER REFERENCE

Blossom Trail (01386 565373, www.blossom-trail.org.uk). British Asparagus Festival (www.britishasparagusfestival.org). Evesham Tourist Information Centre (Almonry Heritage Centre, 01386 446944, www.almonryevesham.org). Evesham Vale Tour Guides (www.eveshamvaletourguides.co.uk). Evesham Vale Light Railway (01386 422282, www.evlr.co.uk). Pershore Tourist Information Centre (01386 556591, www.visitpershore.co.uk).

Shropshire Hills

Romancing the stones.

The Long Mynd and the Stiperstones, Wenlock Edge and Brown Clee: these are the hills of the uncertain borderlands between England and Wales. And though the valleys between the long ridges are rich, lush and romantic, the hilltops are bare and wild, their thin soils supporting little beyond grass and heather. But then, the soil has a right to be exhausted, for this land is almost unimaginably ancient, a relic of a past when only wind and rain moved over the land. Set among the hills are ruined castles and abandoned forts, stone and sod memorials of more violent times. Even the names have a stripped-down feel, with places like Clun and Clee, Sarn and Shelve seemingly worn down to a monosyllabic essence. These hills are a place of deep history.

Nothing expresses this otherness better than the silence and stillness that settles in AE Housman's 'valleys of springs and rivers'. The quietness is strange when you think that this is border country: the numerous castles are testament to the raiders, marauders and armies that passed back and forth across the Marches of England and Wales for centuries. Perhaps what you hear today, when you stare into the star-spattered skies above the hill shadows, is the diminuendo of the clash of arms, the outbreath of a bloody past exhaled into a quiet land.

But the bloody history is matched by a dramatic geography. The Stiperstones and the Long Mynd are parallel ridges, running in a north-easterly direction, with the Mynd pointing like a dagger at the county town of Shrewsbury on the Shropshire plain beyond (Mynd means 'long mountain' and a walk along its seven-mile summit will – eventually – reveal the aptness of its title). A little further east, Wenlock Edge forms another ripple in the land. Brown Clee Hill is the last breaker of what seem like waves rolling off the high mountains of Wales into the English plains. It's a land of fresh horizons, a place of 'high-hilled plains', where a climb to a distant summit might reveal further hidden heights or a sudden and glorious vista into the long valley below.

Since geography is fundamental to the area, it is no surprise that the Shropshire Hills are a geologist's playground: no other comparable area in England has such a variety of rock formations. Stand on the Long Mynd and you stand on rock that formed 565 million years ago. If you could go back to that time, you'd see no animals, no plants, nothing but the bare bones of a planet that is home only to the simplest life forms. For millions of years, the continent that lay behind the Mynd was ground down and washed by rain and wind to the shore, piling up there in layer after layer of sedimentary rock. Then, as the earth stirred in its aeons-long sleep, the rock was squeezed and folded and eventually thrust up.

With its sweeping views and lofty hills, the area around the Long Mynd has been nicknamed 'Little Switzerland'.

They may be all lumped together under the name of the South Shropshire Hills, but each range has a distinctive trait: the Mynd is broad and expansive; Wenlock Edge is covered with trees on its western flank; the Stiperstones cut across Shropshire like a knife, the jagged tors that mark its spine resembling broken-down teeth. The latter were formed during the last Ice Age, when the quartzite ridge that stood above the glaciers was shattered by the extreme temperatures. The explosion produced the Stiperstones trademark scree outcrops, which lend an eerie air to the place – almost imperceptible on a bright summer's day, but when the sun dips behind the Mynd, the shadows darken and mist swirls around the Devil's Chair, it's easy to understand why the Stiperstones is clothed in legend. Mary Webb, whose 1916 novel *The Golden Arrow* was set in the Shropshire Hills, described it thus:

Black, massive, untenanted, yet with a well-worn air. It had the look of a chair from which the occupant had just risen, to which he will shortly return. It was understood that only when vacant could the throne be seen. Whenever rain or driving sleet or mist made a grey shechinah there, people said, 'He is in his chair.'

No doubt the area seemed much more infernal in Victorian times, when it produced one tenth of the nation's lead, and mines, foundries and smelters littered the landscape. Even today, you need to be wary of abandoned mine shafts when venturing off path.

Although much of it is protected, industry still continues on Wenlock Edge, where gravel quarries gnaw away at limestone laid down 450 million years ago when the land lay submerged beneath a shallow tropical sea. Today, Wenlock Edge holds easily recognisable fossilised remains of long-ago coral reefs, some of which resemble a

Brown Clee Hill (above) is the highest point in Shropshire; the view from the Stiperstones (right).

cockle. In fact, so much of the groundwork of modern geology was done on the Edge that a part of the Silurian period, 428 to 423 million years ago, is called the Wenlock Epoch.

This ancient mystique had a profound effect on AE Housman. Writing in the 19th century, the poet felt a deep pull towards these aged hills, and the quiet towns and villages that nestle in their folds. Perhaps it's the contrast between the nakedness of the hills and the lush pastures below that produces the characteristic Salopian tranquillity. As Housman wrote: 'Clunton and Clunbury/Clungunford and Clun/Are the quietest places/Under the sun.' And while there is something almost prelapsarian about the small towns, fields and copses that are clustered in the valleys, the hills that roll above them are a window into a world even more remote.

OTHER BEAUTY SPOTS

The most outlying of Shropshire's hills is the Wrekin, described in Housman's poem 'On Wenlock Edge'. From the Telford side, which most visitors see first, it hardly seems worth a climb – it's just a tree-clad hump with a radio mast jutting out of it. But swing round to the south and you'll see the Wrekin rising proud of the plains, with the more distant hills expanding in a great panorama beyond the flat, fat pastures watered by the River Severn.

The evidence of the area's warlike past is scattered in ruined castles like the one in Clun and, most evocatively, Stokesay Castle. This is the best-preserved fortified manor house in the country, and as you visit it, it is easy to imagine that Laurence of Ludlow, the wool merchant who bought it in 1281, has only just left on one of his trips to Flanders.

WHERE TO STAY & EAT

Set high up on the flanks of the Long Mynd, Jinlye (01694 723243, www.jinlye.co.uk) has mesmerising views and even better walks from the doorstep. The stone guesthouse, built as a crofter's cottage in the 18th century, has wonderful rustic touches, such as beamed ceilings, open log fires and leaded windows.

Clun: 'the quietest place under the sun'.

Just outside Ludlow is Fishmore Hall (01584 875148, www.fishmorehall.co.uk), which was a run-down old reform school before it was turned it into a model boutique hotel. The restaurant is exceptional: chef David Jaram makes the most of excellent local produce, and won Best Sunday Lunch award from the *Observer* Food Awards in 2009.

This highlights the general rule of the area: for dining, head to Ludlow. It's a foodie centre and, exceptionally for a town of its size, has two Michelin-starred restaurants, La Bécasse (01584 872325, www.labecasse.co.uk) and Mr Underhill's (01584 874431, www.mr-underhills.co.uk). The latter is a restaurant with rooms, which are pleasingly plush and tasteful (ask for a room in the annexe on the edge of the river).

For something cheaper, try the Church Inn (01584 872174, www.thechurchinn.com), a traditional pub in the heart of Ludlow, with en suite rooms that do the job just fine.

HOW TO GET THERE

The South Shropshire Hills lie roughly between Shrewsbury and Hereford. **By road** The M54 is the nearest motorway, but the heart of the region – Church Stretton, Craven Arms and Ludlow – lies along the A49. The Stiperstones are accessed by the A488. **By train** Church Stretton, Craven Arms and Ludlow are the nearest stations (National Rail Enquiries, 08457 484950). **By bus** The Shropshire Hills shuttle bus runs on weekends in summer (01743 251000, www.shropshirehillsshuttles.co. uk), connecting Craven Arms, Clun and Bishop's Castle to the Stiperstones, the Long Mynd and Church Stretton. **By bicycle** Wheely Wonderful Cycling (Ludlow, 01568 770755, www.wheely wonderfulcycling.co.uk). **On foot** The car park on the road from Bog to Bridges/Ratlinghope is the starting point for a walk along the Stiperstones. To walk the Long Mynd, you could start at Carding Mill Valley, north of Church Stretton. There's a National Trust visitors' centre and car park there. From Clun, there is an 11-mile walk along the Shropshire Way to the Discovery Centre at Craven Arms. **Map** Ordnance Survey Explorer 217, The Long Mynd & Wenlock Edge; grid ref SO455934.

FURTHER REFERENCE

There are tourist information centres in Church Stretton (01694 723133, www. churchstretton.co.uk), Ironbridge (01952 884391), Ludlow (01584 875053) and Much Wenlock (01952 727679, www. discovershropshire.co.uk), or go to www. visitsouthshropshire.co.uk. See also Shropshire Hills Discovery Centre (01588 676000, www.shropshirehillsdiscovery centre.co.uk), www.shropshirehillsaonb. co.uk and www.walkingbritain.co.uk.

The Roaches

The jagged edge.

Stop giggling at the back there. The name of this craggy escarpment, part of the Staffordshire Peak District, has nothing to do with spliffs or insects. It derives from the French for a rock (*un rocher*), a reference to all the striking millstone grit. That said, the weird and wonderful landscape looks a little trippy, and it's the kind of place that lends itself to mind-bending experiences and spiritual awakenings.

A bleak, jagged outcrop of stone, often shrouded in mist, the Roaches resembles a ridge of petrified surf about to break over the placid Staffordshire farmland below: to the west, as if awaiting the onslaught of this wave of rock, the pleasant wooded valley is neatly walled; to the east, empty tracts of wild peat moorland roll away towards another stone ripple in the landscape, the Ramshaw Rocks. The crest of the Roaches, meanwhile, is studded with two miles of reddish-brown boulders, broken cliffs and mysterious crags; some of the rocks are so outlandish, they appear to belong in the Wild West, rather than the Midlands. On the map, to the south, like the dot of the Roaches' enormous exclamation mark, is Hen Cloud, a lone mini-mountain of looming gritstone.

As befits the hippy name, the Roaches is an eerie, Tolkienesque landscape – in fact, elements of *The Silmarillion*, the author's collection of stories about Middle Earth, were dreamed up in nearby Stafford, as Tolkien recovered from his experiences in the Somme. But the region's association with questing heroes, character being tested and personal growth, go back much further. The area has been identified as the setting for *Sir Gawain and the Green Knight*, that gripping and magical Arthurian romance, written by an anonymous 14th-century poet in West Midlands dialect verse. Translated by Tolkien for broadcast on BBC radio in 1953, it is full of descriptions of this Peak District landscape: 'They [Sir Gawain and his guide] go by banks and by braes where branches are bare/They climb along cliffs where clingeth the cold/The heavens are lifted high, but

The Roaches is known for its strange rock formations; spooky Doxey Pool (below right) is a bottomless lake haunted by a hag; a grouse hides in the heather (top left).

under them evilly/Mist hangs moist on the moor, melts on the mountains/Every hill has a hat, a mist-mantle huge/Brooks break and boil on braes all about/Bright bubbling on their banks where they bustle downwards.' The Roaches themselves put in an appearance: 'A grim place he thought it, and saw no sign of shelter on any side at all/Only high hillsides sheer upon either hand, and notched knuckled crags with gnarled boulders/The very skies by the peaks were scraped, it appeared.'

In real life, the hobbits and knights that dot the fictional landscape have been replaced by rock climbers; in fact, the southern end of the rocks near Windygates is almost too popular in summer. Above the road, up a red sand path lined with rocks and conifers, a cottage carved out of the cliffs doubles as a memorial hut to Don Whillans, a climber of the 1950s, who forged new routes here. Evocatively named climbing trails add to the air of adventure (Perverted Staircase, Demon Wall and Valkyrie). But the summer crowds of climbers are unlikely to match the turnout that greeted the 1872 Royal Visit of the Prince and Princess of Teck. In a scene worthy of *Picnic at Hanging Rock*, the pair ascended to the top, via a staircase cut into the cliff, to the Royal Chair, itself carved out of gritstone. Visitors today can follow in their footstops, no crampons required, for views of Hen Cloud.

From here, a rugged walk along the ridge stretches two miles to the summit, the wind buffeting the piles of stone and bending the wide swathes of heather. The ascent is

There are sweeping views of the placid Staffordshire farmland, and Tittesworth Reservoir, from the top of the Roaches.

interrupted halfway by the spooky black water of Doxey Pool. Though no bigger than a tennis court, legend has it that it's bottomless, and haunted by a hag called Jenny Greenteeth, who drags passers-by into its depths. On a sunny day, however, it's not creepy at all. And beyond Doxey Pool, sweeping vistas open up westwards towards the hills of Wales and north to the giant Lovell Telescope at Jodrell Bank.

At a dawdling pace, it takes an hour to reach the summit. But to echo Sir Gawain's journey of self-discovery, you must continue to walk on two miles past the peak, north-west to Lud's Church. This mysterious woodland chasm is thought to be the inspiration for the Green Chapel, the site of Sir Gawain's famous duel with the Green Knight. Hidden in the bosky hillside below the ridge, the lush, ancient ravine is oh-so-quiet, yet it has an indefinable aura of menace. The towering walls are covered in virulent green moss, the muddy bottom is dark and dank, and the air is still; after the open and windy wonders of the ridge, it feels vaguely disturbing. Not somewhere you'd want to end up late at night, and the floor of the chasm gets little light even during the day. As Tolkien's translation puts it: 'It had a hole at the end and at either side/and with grass in green patches was grown all over/and was all hollow within: nought but an old cavern/or a cleft in an old crag... "Here the Devil might say, I ween/his matins about midnight"!'

Dramatic stuff, but then Gawain had an appointment here with a not-very-jolly green giant ready to chop his head off – not exactly your average walk in the countryside. It makes you wonder what that poet was smoking.

OTHER BEAUTY SPOTS

The Roaches sit on the northwestern extremity of the Staffordshire Moorlands. Dubbed the 'West Virginia of the North Midlands' by Matthew Parris in *The Times*, it does indeed possess a bluegrass, backward charm. The region also boasts the highest village pub in the UK. Standing at an altitude of 1,518-feet, the New Inn is in a place called Flash, but this simple moorlands drinking hole is anything but. Three Shires Head, two miles north of Flash, is a remote and twisted valley complex where Staffordshire, Derbyshire and Cheshire meet in a secluded limestone gulch, with a small river running through the rough moorland. This hidden pocket was once the haunt of smugglers, who could nip over the border into a neighbouring county when the law came calling. Here you'll find Panniers Pool Bridge, a 400-year-old stone arch above a waterfall and the dark River Dane.

The Dane Valley Way is a 40-mile path between Buxton and Middlewich that takes in open fields, rocky quarries, boggy moors, deciduous woodland and the River Dane. Below Lud's Church, the Dane is joined by the Black Brook at a lovely spot overhung by beech trees. The Hanging Stone, a *Flintstones*-style rock formation, is a landmark on the path from Lud's Church to Danebridge; it has been inscribed with a memorial to Henry Brocklehurst, once the local landowner, who was killed in action in Burma in 1942. Goldsitch Moss and Blackbank Valley Nature Reserve is dotted with pink gritstone outcrops above acres of heather, pine woodland and swathes of spongey sphagnum moss, with tremendous views of the Roaches. Superb views over the Ramshaw Rocks and the Roaches, revealing the hobbit-like quality of the landscape, can also be had from the moors around the Mermaid Inn, a remote pub on the road northwest of Thorncliffe.

WHERE TO STAY & EAT

In Leek, the Peak Weavers Rooms & Restaurant (01538 383729, www.peakweavers hotel.co.uk) is an elegant Georgian building with six neat bedrooms and an award-winning restaurant. Nearer the rocks themselves, in Blackshaw Moor, the Three Horseshoes Inn & Country Hotel (01538 300296, www.3shoesinn.co.uk) has a gorgeous garden with moorland views, and 26 comfortable rooms in a faux period style.

Adventurous options include the YHA Gradbach Mill (0845 371 9118, www.yha.org. uk), a mill conversion on the River Dane. Its riverside café is open at summer lunchtimes, hearty evening meals are served, and double rooms are available. Under the Roaches, Rock Hall is a stone cottage that is also the Don Whillans Memorial Hut (you must join the British Mountaineering Council to stay here, see www.thebmc.co.uk).

The Roaches Tea Rooms in Upper Hulme (01538 300345, www.roaches tearooms.co.uk) is the nearest spot for a cup of tea, a Staffordshire oatcake or a home-made meal. The nearest pub to the Roaches is Ye Olde Rock Inn (Upper Hulme, 01538 300324), where hikers and climbers sup real ales. Further north, the Ship Inn (Wincle, Cheshire, 01260 227217), a 16th-century pub, does British comfort food (fried lamb kidneys on black pudding, steak and ale pie) in a charming setting above the River Dane.

HOW TO GET THERE

The Roaches lie in Staffordshire four miles north of Leek and 12 miles southwest of Buxton. **By road** Take the A53 between Leek and Buxton, turning off at Upper Hulme. **By train** Buxton rail station (National Rail Enquiries, 08457 484950. **By bus** A daily bus service (118) between Hanley (Stoke-on-Trent) and Sheffield calls at Blackshaw Moor, near the Three Horseshoes Inn. There is also a bus service from Stoke to Leek (D&G Bus, 01782 332337, www.dgbus. co.uk; First, 01782 592500, www.first group.com). **On foot** Walk one (five miles): start at the car park below Rockhall. Climb to the ridge of the Roaches, on to the summit, and continue in a loop from Bearstone Rock beyond (at the northern tip of the ridge) to the Hanging Stone and back via Lud's Church. Walk two (four miles): start at Roach End (near Bearstone Rock) and make for the summit of the Roaches, then continue along the ridge to Rockhall, and beyond on to Hen Cloud if you're feeling fit. **Map** Ordnance Survey Explorer OL24, The Peak District; grid ref SK001638.

FURTHER REFERENCE

Leek Tourist Information Centre (01538 483741, www.enjoystaffordshire.com).

Lathkill Dale

Small wonder.

It's hard not to fall in love with the Derbyshire Dales. There's a personable feel to these steep, wooded river valleys, which twist through high acres of green farmland in the middle of England. Hidden away but readily approachable, they're some of the most adorable tracts of deep countryside in Britain, with their clear streams, dappled woodlands and rocky flourishes. There are at least a score of separate dales, major and minor, an extraordinary series of craggy, tree-filled gulches scattered across the Peak District National Park. The southern section is known as the White Peak, thanks to its pale grey limestone; the northern part, Dark Peak, is characterised by forbidding millstone grit. In the heart of the former lies Lathkill, the most enticing dale of all. A cosy river valley, it is blessed with trout-filled rivers, wild-flower meadows, rugged rocks and ruined mines.

Part of its charm is its size: Lathkill is almost a dale in miniature. Just over three miles from end to end, it's easily walked in a couple of hours. The tiny river Lathkill itself is only five miles long when in full winter flow, gushing out of a cave near the top of the dale, then babbling down eastward to meet the River Wye. And though it is a stone's throw from the well-known town of Bakewell, Lathkill Dale is discreet, easily missed by passing traffic.

This verdant cleft in the landscape nurtures flora and fauna galore. Some of these are rare, hence the acronyms and accolades: it's a Site of Special Scientific Interest (SSSI), owing to its acidic lowland grassland and rich woodland, and a Special Area of Conservation (SAC), thanks to its wildlife and ravine forests of ash, wych elm and lime.

But it's the intriguing rocky landscape that lends Lathkill a distinctive flavour. The weathered limestone cliffs set the craggy tone, stacked up in layers along the lip of the

Lathkill Dale is sprinkled with rocks and streams.

dale and topped by the odd wind-battered tree. Just below them, the steep grassy slopes are broken up by scree and scrub; on the floor of the dale, the small river flows quietly around large mossy boulders.

The industrial detritus that comes with the terrain – abandoned mine shafts and grassy spoil heaps – strangely enriches the landscape, instead of scarring it. Ricklow Quarry, at the top of the dale near the lead-mining village of Monyash, once produced 'grey marble', a pale limestone that was used to build grand houses in the area, including Chatsworth. Today, its towering grey slabs reveal sections of a marine shelf-reef, formed 360 million years ago when England was near the Equator. The immaculate condition of the fossils suggests that the warm, prehistoric seas here were once shallow and calm.

The view of the dale from the quarry issues a charming invitation: steep hillsides tumbling into a narrow, densely wooded gorge. Cales Dale, to the south-east, is another stony spectacle – great grey wrinkly rocks ('limestone karst') that are fissured like an elephant's skin. But it's got a pretty side too: glorious hay meadows, found above One Ash Grange Farm. Scattered around Lathkill Dale like confetti, these meadows are a mosaic of wild-flowers in spring and summer. Whimsical names accompany the 40 species that proliferate here: flowering pignut and moonwort ferns, harebells and fairy flax, mountain currants and mouse-ear hawkweed. Jacob's Ladder, or *polemonium caeruleum*, a rare type of phlox, flourishes on the damper, north-facing slopes in June.

Downstream from Cales Dale, shady woodland frames the river as it trickles through reedbeds and ponds, over weirs and small waterfalls, entering the Derbyshire Dales National Nature Reserve below Mill Farm. On the opposite bank, in Meadow Place Wood, there are fleeting and fluttering glimpses of wagtails, redstarts, woodpeckers and spotted flycatchers. Near the waterfalls, twitchers keep their eyes peeled – and camera lenses trained – for a sighting of a dipper, the UK's only all-singing, all-diving songbird. Other A-list celebrities of the dale include two elusive butterflies – the white-letter hairstreak and brown argus – and the water vole.

Although devastated nationwide by the predations of American mink, water voles thrive in Lathkill – one of the last bastions of the swimming rodent anthropomorphised as Ratty in *The Wind in the Willows*. Another native river-dweller that was nearly wiped out by a Yankee invader is the white-clawed crayfish, but a new population is taking hold.

Indeed, nature has a way of taking over here: the mossy ruins of stone-built industrial workings seem to have merged with the old woods near Over Haddon. But

Bateman's House, named after the speculator who went bankrupt attempting to extract galena (lead ore) from these riverbanks in the 19th century, still has its old steps into the shaft where a massive steam-pumping engine once drained the Mandale lead mines.

Lead has been mined in nearby Over Haddon, the tidy little village overlooking the dale, since Roman times. But, more recently, it was the scene of an abortive Victorian gold rush (it was, in the end, fool's gold). These days, visitors to Lathkill search for natural treasures more various and fleeting than those heavy metals.

OTHER BEAUTY SPOTS

Lathkill is in the middle of the Derbyshire Dales, which are famous for their dramatic cliffs, jagged rocks and pure rivers. The area's most famous regions lie to the north (Monsal, Chee, Monk's, Tideswell) and south (Dove Dale and Ilam, near Ashbourne).

Arbor Low stone circle, south of Monyash, offers a full helping of Lathkill limestone and is one of the most important Neolithic henge monuments in the north of England. It consists of 50 great chunks of limestone, lying flat. Like most stone circles, it gives sweeping views across the countryside.

Two of the county's great houses are also nearby: Chatsworth, the palatial residence of the Duke of Devonshire, where the manicured parkland is open all year; and Haddon Hall, described by Simon Jenkins as 'the most perfect English house to survive from the Middle Ages'. It's a popular location for films and TV, complete with a walled garden stepping down to the river Wye.

Like the disused mines, the Headstone Viaduct of the old Midland Railway is another man-made spectacle that blends in to the scenery – in this case, in Monsal Dale. Its construction in 1863 was famously seen as an act of vandalism on the landscape by John Ruskin, who wrote 'now, every fool in Buxton can be in Bakewell in half an hour, and every fool in Bakewell at Buxton'. Not by train they can't, these days, though Peak Rail chugs along part of the old line from Matlock to Rowsley, from where there's a riverside walk up the west bank of the Derwent to Chatsworth.

WHERE TO STAY & EAT

Part of the Haddon Hall Estate, the Peacock at Rowsley (01629 733518, www.the peacockatrowsley.com) is a 17th-century manor house that has been converted into a boutique hotel. The rooms are individually styled; the best ones overlook the garden, as does the panelled dining room, which serves sophisticated, locally sourced fare (Derbyshire beef with pearl barley, leek, red wine sauce and snails, for instance). The hotel is also famous for trout fishing on the Wye. The Lathkil Hotel (01629 812501, www.lathkil.co.uk)

is a popular pub in Over Haddon, with a good variety of real ales and ambitious pub food (venison and blackberry casserole, baked rainbow trout). The four bedrooms seem pretty basic for the price, but some overlook the Dale – a view worth paying for.

In Monyash, the Bulls Head (01629 812372) is a sturdy, old-fashioned village hostelry with a few inexpensive rooms and antique fittings in the bar. Also in Monyash, the Old Smithy Tearooms and Restaurant (01629 810190, www.oldsmithymonyash. piczo.com), serves all-day breakfasts, coffee and cakes – ('muddy boots welcome') – and opens on Saturday evenings. The George Hotel (01629 636292) in Youlgreave, is a reliable, down-to-earth hikers' hotel, with proper fry-ups. The Youlgreave YHA (0845 3719151, www.yha.org.uk) is full of character, and has a good café.

The river trickles over weirs and small waterfalls.

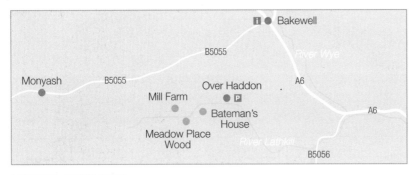

HOW TO GET THERE

Lathkill Dale is in Derbyshire, 1.5 miles south-west of Bakewell, ten miles west of Chesterfield. **By road** The M1 is the nearest motorway, but the heart of the region – Matlock, Bakewell, Buxton – lies along the A6. From the M1, take Junction 28 to join the A38 towards Derby. Then take the A610 towards Matlock, followed by the A6. From Bakewell, take the B5055 to Monyash. Over Haddon, above the middle of the dale, is signposted left off the Monyash road after a mile. **By train** Matlock rail station (National Rail Enquiries, 08457 484950). From Matlock Riverside station, Peak Rail (www.peakrail.co.uk) runs steam and diesel trains on a four-mile restored section of track, up to Rowsley. **By bus** Eight bus services a day link Bakewell with Over Haddon and Monyash during the week; services are less frequent on weekends (0871 2002233, www.traveline.org.uk or derbysbus.info). **On foot** There are marked walking trails along the dale from Over Haddon and Monyash, with various footpaths branching off the long-distance Limestone Way between Monyash and Youlgreave. Mill Farm is a good access point to the middle of the dale, halfway between Over Haddon and Monyash. **Map** Ordnance Survey Explorer OL24, The Peak District; grid ref SK184658.

FURTHER REFERENCE

There are tourist information centres in Bakewell (01629 813227) and Matlock (01629 583388). For both, see www. visitpeakdistrict.com. The Lathkill Dale Geology Trail (www.naturalengland.org. uk) goes from Over Haddon to Monyash.

Farndale

Mellow yellow.

The daffodils that inspired Wordsworth's famous poem of 1804 grew near Ullswater in the Lake District. ('I wander'd lonely as a cloud/That floats on high o'er vales and hills/When all at once I saw a crowd/A host, of golden daffodils'.) But his expressive, eloquent musings could equally have applied to the valley of Farndale, in North York Moors National Park. Here, thousands of wild daffodils blanket the ground from late March till early April, when walkers descend to celebrate the arrival of spring. But the locals are not quite as lyrical about this extraordinary sight as Wordsworth was: 'Grand, eh?' said one burly man as he photographed his companion in front of the golden display that lines the Farndale Daffodil Trail. When asked if he'd like his picture taken with his companion, he joked: 'Nay... Her husband might find out about us then.'

His genial, witty response sums up the North Yorkshire scenery perfectly: rough and welcoming. The rough part consists of high, untamed, heather-covered moors of raw beauty and strange, eerie landscapes characterised by the remains of prehistoric settlements and ferocious storms – these are the Yorkshire Moors of our imagination, of Heathcliff-esque terrain, all brooding beauty and aching melodrama. The welcoming part of the scenery is where Farndale comes in: a haven of lush and friendly rolling valleys, where centuries of low-maintenance farming have shaped a countryside that is gentle and hospitable to both nature and visitors (especially ones with ageing knees). It's tame and peaceful here – Heathcliff gone soft, if you will.

Or so it would seem, from the well-tended and well-trodden, one-and-a-half mile Daffodil Trail between Low Mill and Church Houses, a short path that attracts 40,000 visitors each April, all here to see the same thing: the swathes of yellow that brighten up the gentle, light-dappled woodland and line the shores of the meandering River Dove.

And these aren't just any old daffodils. The *Narcissi pseudonarcissus*, or wild daffodil, is a smaller, increasingly rare and more fragile species than the common variety, and it blooms later in the season. Purists prefer the delicate gold and lemon flower because it's supposedly native to Britain (the medieval Cistercian monks at nearby Rievaulx Abbey were thought to have planted them en masse in these parts, hence their other name, Lenten Lilies), but others say the Romans brought them to this country. However they got here, they are scattered in their thousands along the banks of the Dove. It is a pleasing spectacle, particularly on a spring day, when the massed ranks of yellow-headed soldiers sway gently in the breeze as though at ease after a regimental parade. But the atmosphere is not always so pastoral: if you come at the height of the season, on a busy day, and walk the main trail, the sheer number of people calls to mind summer in a local park, particularly when you reach the Daffy Caffy café at the hamlet of Church Houses, where everyone stops for a cake and a cuppa, or the Feversham Arms pub, further on.

But nirvana is not far away. After you walk the main trail, instead of retracing your steps south back to the car park at Low Mill, venture east through a bridlegate, and follow the upper path for a couple of miles across the moor. You'll hardly encounter a soul as you tramp across the farmland. Away from the daffodil-snapping hordes, you get a real sense of the way this delightful valley has evolved – slowly and considerately. The patchwork quilt of fields and hills is criss-crossed with traditional Yorkshire drystone walls, which enclose cows and sheep; the farmyard machinery is decidedly old-school; mobiles don't work; electricity is a relatively recent arrival, and the issue of broadband is still being debated in the village hall. As you close the gates behind you, and gaze down across the valley, you realise that it is possible for man and nature to coexist in harmony. Nature may have laid the foundations of the landscape, when melting glaciers carved the valley during the last Ice Age, but the gentle, old-fashioned farming methods have allowed the daffodils to thrive here. No fertilisers are used; once the flowers have bloomed, farmers let their stock in to graze and deadhead the flowers, strengthening the bulbs for the next year. The birdsong is all the sweeter for lack of chemicals: meadow pipits, golden plover, curlew, lapwing and grouse positively flourish in the farmland and moors around Farndale.

But if you yearn for even more nature, and less of the man-made, there's yet another part of Farndale that nobody tells you about – a secret daffodil trail that has eluded the happy snappers. The Moors Bus doesn't stop there, there are no loos, you won't find an information caravan, much less a Daffy Caff. Close to Lowna Bridge, which crosses the gurgling Dove in the village of Gillamoor, this wooded dirt track forms a wild daffodil trail that's worlds away from its genteel northern counterpart. It's a mix of mud, water, daffodils, rough terrain and a barely-there footpath that follows the river north all the way back to Low Mill – sometimes clambering up the valley and away from the river to offer enchanting views, sometimes clinging to the banks, all the while serving up sheets of yellow for your eyes only. It's a magical, seven-mile walk, there and back.

Yet look closely, and man's careful hand is still evident amid the wilderness: a wall-enclosed Quaker burial ground is the scenic resting place for 114 souls buried here between 1675 and 1837; the rickety, wooden Dale End Bridge is a good viewpoint for taking in all the flower power; and an atmospheric, disused quarry on Rudland Rigg – at the top of a steep trail – leads on to Harland Moor, where the horizons stretch forever.

Even when the daffodils aren't blooming, beauty abounds here: after the narcissi have passed their peak, thousands of bluebells erupt from a white carpet of wood anemones, framed by brilliant white blackthorns in bloom. Throughout it all, the birds chirp, play and court each other, and inspire romantic souls to do the same. Wordsworth would have been impressed.

OTHER BEAUTY SPOTS

In a secluded valley, the village of Rosedale Abbey is a starting point for walks across lonely moors and romantic landscapes characterised by rushing rivers and crumbling farmhouses. The route over the moors to Lastingham leads to tiny St Mary's church, with its impressive Norman crypt. The landscape on most of these walks is wilder and more desolate than at Farndale.

Rosedale's short Mines and Kilns walk is dotted with industrial ruins. But you can also hire clubs and play a round of golf at the prettiest (and hilliest) golf course in the country (01751 417270, www.rosedaleabbeygolf.co.uk). Stock up on a picnic with old-school cakes such as coconut pyramids at the Abbey Tea Room and Store (01751 417475, www.abbeytearoom.co.uk) beforehand.

The ridiculously picturesque Hutton-le-Hole is also a starting point for walks, but linger in the village too. With sheep roaming the streets and green in the hope of picking up scraps from picnickers lazing by the stream, this is north Yorkshire at its loveliest.

Nearby Helmsley is bigger but equally handsome. If you don't feel like tackling the 110-mile Cleveland Way, which crosses the moors and ends in Filey on the Yorkshire coast, there's an eye-opening, three-mile sampler: from Helmsley Castle, a majestic medieval fortress, to the atmospheric ruin of Rievaulx Abbey.

Daffodils line the banks of the River Dove. The peak display is usually from late March until mid-April, but it varies every year.

WHERE TO STAY & EAT

The Feversham Arms Hotel (Helmsley, 01439 770766, www.fevershamarmshotel.com) is a stylish and relaxing base for the North Yorkshire Moors. Calm aching limbs after a hike with a swim in the outdoor pool or a treatment in the Verbena Spa. A charming Helmsley alternative is the No. 54 B&B (01439 771533, www.number54.co.uk), a pretty, country-style affair, from the flagstone floors to the home-baked muffins.

For dinner, the Feversham Arms Hotel has an elegant but unstuffy dining room. For lunch, the rustic Lion Inn (Blakey Ridge, 01751 417320, www.lionblakey.co.uk) offers hearty fare and views from the highest point on the North Yorkshire Moors (1,300 feet). It also offers B&B. Michelin-starred food is served at the Star Inn at Harome (01439 770397, www.thestaratharome.co.uk); the chef Andrew Pern's autobiography, *Black Pudding and Foie Gras*, sums up his homely but upmarket menu. On the daffodil trail, the Feversham Arms Inn (01751 433206, www.fevershamarmsinn.co.uk) does pub grub and B&B.

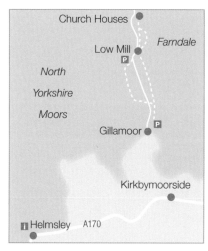

HOW TO GET THERE

Farndale is between Bransdale and Rosedale, five miles north of Kirkbymoorside, in the North York Moors National Park. **By road** From the A19 take the A170 to Helmsley and Kirbymoorside and follow signs to Hutton-le-Hole, and from there to Low Mill for the Daffodil Trail. For the longer, wilder walk, go to Gillamoor. **By train** GNER and Virgin trains to York (08457 484950, www.nationalrail.co.uk), then bus. **By bus** Connect with cross-country bus services into Helmsley (0871 200 2233, www.yorkshiretravel.net). In summer, and on Sundays and Bank Holidays (April to October), the Moorsbus service (01845 597000, www.visitthe moors.co.uk/moorsbus) links local villages, with a Farndale Daffodil Shuttle Bus operating between Hutton-le-Hole car park and Low Mill in peak daffodil season. **On foot** For the short Farndale walk, parking and an information point are available at Low Mill. To do the long walk – the secret, wild daffodil trail – limited parking is available in the layby near Lowna Bridge in Gillamoor, south of Low Mill. It is possible to do both walks in a single, 12-mile loop. Daffodils are usually out from late March till mid-April. **Map** Ordnance Survey Explorer OL26, North York Moors; grid ref SE680943.

FURTHER REFERENCE

There is a tourist office in Helmsley (01439 770173, www.ryedale.gov.uk). For more, see also www.farndale.org/index1.htm, www.northyorkmoors.org.uk, www.yorkshire.com, www.walkingenglishman.com.

Upper Teesdale

Wild flowers and waterfalls.

Most people associate the River Tees with the grim industrial landscape of Middlesbrough, but go 70 miles upstream, and it's a very different story. Upper Teesdale, near the source of the Tees, is a landscape of wild flowers and waterfalls, fells and dales, hay meadows and heather-topped moors. This unsung corner of north-east England is part of the Durham Dales, the lesser-known sibling of the Yorkshire Dales, its neighbour to the south. But Teesdale is no poor relation when it comes to natural assets – indeed, it falls in the North Pennines Area of Outstanding Natural Beauty. When the great fell walker and guidebook author Alfred Wainwright wrote his classic Pennine Way Companion in 1968, he described the waterfalls and river gorge around High Force as 'near perfection' – high praise for a writer who chose his adjectives sparingly. High above the hay meadows, the scars of Holwick Fell guard some of Britain's most bleakly beautiful and remote moorland.

It may not yet be a household name, but Upper Teesdale is known to naturalists. Botanists can identify the rare wildflowers – Teesdale violets, mountain pansy, early marsh orchids and bird's-eye primrose. Birders keep their eyes on the sky for curlews, lapwings, skylarks and rare black grouse. Geologists ponder the distinctive chunky rocks that form the river canyon, the Whin Sill; they are similar to the Giant's Causeway in Ulster, and, at 295 million years, just as old.

But the flowers steal the show. In April and May, rare alpine varieties appear; from June to mid-July, the hay meadows bloom with a technicolour blanket of wild flowers and grasses. The richest meadows can have more than 30 different species of flower per square metre, including the evocatively named wood crane's bill, ragged robin, yellow rattle and adder's tongue fern. This profusion and diversity are hallmarks of traditional hay meadows, which have been left untouched by artificial fertiliser. These precious meadows have all but disappeared in Britain, a casualty of intensive farming techniques; only four square miles remain, almost half of them in the North Pennines.

Hannah's Meadow, north of Cotherstone, is one of the loveliest hay meadows, but it has cultural significance too. It was once home to Hannah Hauxwell, who appeared in the 1973 television documentary *Too Long a Winter*. Gentle, serene and unworldly, this white-haired farmer captivated audiences with her harsh and solitary life – she lived without electricity or running water on remote Low Birk Hatt farm. An ailing Hannah left in 1988, trading austerity for a cosy cottage in Cotherstone, but the farm still stands beside Blackton Reservoir. It's easy to see why she didn't go far. In early summer, when the globeflowers and wood anemones bloom and the meadow foxtail and sweet vernal grasses sway in the breeze, Hannah's Meadow is glorious.

Below the hay meadows, wild flowers also abound along the River Tees. Scramble down through marsh marigold, bluebell, wild raspberry, orchid and wild garlic to the river's edge. In spring or summer, plot your way to a rock in the middle of the water, where you can picnic or daydream as the river tumbles past in a chaotic jumble of cataracts or settles in deep, peaty pools. It is a mesmerising setting, your solitude disturbed only by a white-chested dipper whirring by or the yellow streak of a grey wagtail.

The cataracts are a prelude to a spectacular trio of waterfalls: the escalating grandeur of Low Force; the tumultuous power of High Force and the snarling Cauldron Snout, all lying within six miles of each other. Low Force wins the beauty contest, with its rocky staircase of endless falls and tree-lined banks. You can rock-hop to a pair of wooded islands surrounded by rushing river. Nearby is another Teesdale botanical rarity, England's largest juniper wood. There, High Force makes itself heard – first as a growl, then a low rumble, and finally a thunderous roar.

It is a magnificent sight. High Force may not the highest waterfall in England, although it has a sheer 70-foot drop. But measured by strength and volume, it is the biggest: hundreds of tons of white foam power through a cleft between columns of black rock to the swirling water below. In winter, a second fall doubles the drama.

The third great Tees waterfall is Cauldron Snout. The longest in England, it crashes brutally through a narrow gorge for 650 feet, its power matched by the wildness of the landscape. It lies above the tree line, beyond the last whitewashed farmstead, in the remote High Pennines. So it comes as a surprise to be confronted with a man-made reservoir

dam and a distant white radome that looks like a golf ball and monitors transatlantic air traffic from high on Great Dun Fell.

Cow Green Reservoir was built in 1969 to supply water for Teesside's industries. It was the site of one of the first green protests, when environmentalists fought to save nature's splendour from oblivion. The conservation battle was lost, but volunteers painstakingly dug up the rare plants and relocated them to the Moor House-Upper Teesdale National Nature Reserve, a mile west of Cauldron Snout.

High up in the Pennines, this is England's largest nature reserve (at 33 square miles), a UNESCO reserve and a wild-flower wonder. The combination of its subarctic climate (it can snow here in June) and sugar limestone soil has produced the Teesdale Assemblage, a precious collection of tiny alpine flowers: mountain pansies, Teesdale violets, nodding cowslips and bird's eye primrose. They bloom in late spring among grass nibbled by Swaledale sheep.

The reserve hosts another natural spectacle: England's endangered black grouse. But one must rise early to see them at their best. After dawn in April, up to 30 cocky males congregate at Langdon Beck to fan out their white tail feathers and seduce females.

This is as remote as England gets. Beyond Cronkley Fell, the land feels truly wild. No population, no farms, no walls, no roads, no light pollution, just miles of nothingness stretching into Cumbria. Yet there's one more surprise. Amid all this daunting vastness is a tiny piece of delicate glory: barely two centimetres across, the spring gentian is a big deal among British botanists. You might see it growing in the Alps or on the Burren on the west coast of Ireland, but in Britain, you will find it only in Upper Teesdale, particularly around Cronkley and Widdybank Fells, where it blooms in May. Its electric-blue petals leave a lasting impression – a bit like Upper Teesdale.

Low Force (previous page) is one of three waterfalls in Upper Teesdale; Cauldron Snout (below) is the longest waterfall in England. Wild flowers thrive in the hay meadows here; the spring gentian, a brilliant blue rarity, blooms on the higher fells.

OTHER BEAUTY SPOTS

Utterly remote, High Cup Nick, beyond Cow Green Reservoir, is a deep, straight and dramatic gorge, a giant's bowling alley – and one of the most impressive glacial valleys in England, studded with striking grey dolerite crags.

Hamsterley Forest, between the Wear and Tees valleys, has 5,000 acres of broadleaved and coniferous woodland. Managed by the Forestry Commission, it is sprinkled with cycle paths, riding trails and waymarked walks.

Fish for native brown trout at Balderhead, Cow Green and Selset reservoirs. In desolate moorland fells, these are three of the finest – and prettiest – wild trout fisheries in the country. Fishing permits for Cow Green from honesty box on site; for Balderhead and Selset, from Grassholme Visitors Centre (01833 641121).

WHERE TO STAY & EAT

Boutique hotels and gastropubs haven't yet reached Upper Teesdale. Many B&Bs are stuck in the era of nylon bedspread and woodchip wallpaper, with meals a matter of basic refuelling. But there are exceptions, like the Rose and Crown at Romaldkirk (01833 650213, www.rose-and-crown.co.uk). The perfect country inn, it has 12 stylish bedrooms, a characterful old bar and an elegant panelled dining room, which serves excellent regional specialties such as Woodalls Cumberland ham and honey roast figs, Cotherstone cheese soufflé and Teesdale lamb.

The Langdon Beck Hotel (01833 622267, www.langdonbeckhotel.com) couldn't be more different. This remote real-ale pub has seven simple bedrooms, and such basic fare as ham and eggs. But the fine views, homespun geological museum and friendly welcome make up for its lack of surface glamour.

At Cotherstone, the Fox & Hounds (01833 650241, www.cotherstonefox.co.uk) does decent pub grub, while Middleton in Teesdale has Brunswick House (01833 640393, www.brunswickhouse.net), a smart and comfortable B&B that also serves dinner.

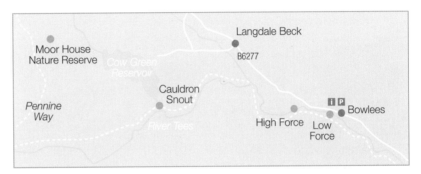

HOW TO GET THERE

Upper Teesdale lies in Durham west of Middlesbrough. **By car** Access from the A1 and M6. The A66 passes the southern edge of Teesdale. Nearest towns are Barnard Castle, Middleton in Teesdale and Cotherstone. For the waterfalls, take the B6277 to Bowlees Visitor Centre and walk, or drive to High Force, five miles west of Middleton in Teesdale. Park at the High Force Hotel and pay £2 and £1.50 entrance fee. **By train** Darlington is the nearest station (National Rail Enquiries, 08457 484950). **By bus** Local Arriva services from Darlington to Barnard Castle and Middleton in Teesdale (0871 200 2233, www.arrivabus.co.uk). **On foot** For the river Tees and Low Force, start at Bowlees Visitors Centre. Cross the road and walk through Bank Farm. Cross the Tees at Scorberry Bridge and take the Pennine Way footpath north to Wynch Bridge. Continue on the Pennine Way to see High Force from above. The low access to High Force is from the opposite bank, signposted on the B6277. The Pennine Way continues west to Cauldron Snout, Cow Green Reservoir and Moor House NNR. To view the Baldersdale hay meadows, turn west off the B6277 north of Cotherstone, take the country lane by the Hury Reservoir. **Map** Ordnance Survey Explorer OL31, North Pennines; grid ref NY905285.

FURTHER REFERENCE

Bowlees Visitors Centre and Low Force, Bowlees (01833 622292, closed weekdays Nov-Mar). Cow Green Reservoir and Cauldron Snout, part of Moor House-Upper Teesdale National Nature Reserve (01833 622374, guided walks available). Hannah's Meadow Nature Reserve (0191 584 3112, www.wildlifetrusts.org). High Force (01833 622209, www.rabycastle.com). North Pennines AONB (01388 528801, www.northpennines.org.uk).

Ullswater

A lake for all seasons.

The Lake District National Park has a lake for every season and sensibility. There's forbidding Wastwater, the deepest and most desolate lake, and the photogenic Tarn Hows, a calendar staple. Windermere, the biggest lake, is the most popular with tourists. Derwentwater, dubbed the 'Queen of the Lakes', is the pretty one, loved for its oak-lined shores and tempting islands. Lonely Innominate Tarn, high on Haystacks, is so atmospheric that the walker and guidebook author Alfred Wainwright had his ashes scattered here. But Ullswater, lying amid the park's far eastern fells, would arguably win the Lake District beauty contest.

It's got the lot. Seven miles of gently zigzagging, sparkling lake; heathered crags and heady peaks; tiny islands and sandy coves; tumbling waterfalls and timeless secluded valleys; red-funnelled steamers and unspoiled walkers' bars, and even a touch of Wordsworth – he wrote 'Daffodils' after visiting Ullswater.

Its beauty is varied. The lake looks deceptively benign at Pooley Bridge, at the north-eastern corner. But as the quiet back road winds south along its eastern shoreline, the fells gradually reveal themselves in all their grandeur: Hallin Fell, which overlooks the one-hotel hamlet of Howtown, was once scorned by Wainwright as a climb for 'sandals and slippers and polished shoes', but, at 1,271 feet, it's not exactly a walk in the park, and the view impresses whatever your footwear; Place Fell, which towers 2,154 feet to the south-east, has vistas to the high drama of Striding Edge (a sharp ridge), and Helvellyn, the third-highest peak in lakeland (3,117 feet).

Beneath such powerful backdrops lie classic scenes of English pleasantness: farmsteads of grey Cumberland slate or pristine whitewashed cottages; old gabled boathouses with mossy roofs that suggest a moonlit row. Hardy Herdwick sheep make precipitous tracks between lichen-covered drystone walls. Woods of oak, ash and silver birch are reflected on the lake in a scene that has proved irresistible to poets and artists, from the sublime (Wordsworth and JMW Turner) to the awful (the tourist tat that fills the gift shops of Glenridding).

Indeed, the word 'picturesque' might have been invented for Ullswater. William Gilpin, the 19th-century Cumbrian clergyman, artist and teacher, first popularised the term when trying to define the lakes' beauty, and nowhere could be more picturesque than Ullswater on a clear, blue sunny day.

Yet this wouldn't be the Lake District if it didn't rain – and when it rains here, it pours. Frequently. When the sunshine is switched off, it is overtaken by leaden skies and swirling mists that obliterate the fells and add a sense of mystery and danger (the Patterdale Mountain Rescue team is one of Britain's most called-out volunteer emergency services). Sometimes it seems that the rain will never end, but it often stops as quickly as it began – and it's back to the water.

Ullswater is a sailor's lake. Thanks to a 10mph speed limit, there are no noisy speedboats or waterskiers, only the little puttering blue-and-white motorboats for hire from St Patrick's boatyard at Glenridding. Less intrusive still are the *Swallows and Amazons*-style, red-sailed dinghies, or the varnished wooden rowing boats that ply the lake on balmy summer days.

The showboats, in fair weather or foul, are the 'steamers' (they are actually powered by diesel these days) of the Ullswater Steam Navigation Company. Founded in 1855 to transport passengers and provisions up and down the lake, they make for an elegant, nostalgic cruise, with their red funnels and pale green livery, evocative names (*Lady of the Lake*, *Raven*) and departure points from wooden piers.

Cruising and walking go together at Ullswater. The low-level footpath along the Ullswater's eastern shore runs between Glenridding and Howtown, both departure points for steamers. This allows walkers to make one leg of their journey by boat, which is a good idea: at six miles, and often rocky underfoot, this path – one of the best-loved walks in the lakes – is more than a gentle stroll, and on a hot day, the wooded sections and streams are blessedly welcome.

Along the way, the grassy promontory of Silver Point is a panoramic spot for a picnic: behind you, the lower slopes of Birk Fell are clothed in fern and foxglove, and a rocky outcrop erupts with purple heather; straight ahead is tiny Norfolk island; on the opposite shore stand Great Dodd and Great Mell Fell. The combination of lake, island, fells and sky is enough to inspire poetry, and it has: at Glencoyne Bay, on 15 April 1802, Dorothy Wordsworth, William's sister, came across that famous bank of daffodils. In her journal she wrote of them 'resting their heads upon these stones as on a pillow for weariness, and the rest tossed and reeled and danced and seemed as if they verily laughed with the wind that blew upon them over the lake'. Two years later, William wrote his poem.

Sandwick, north of Silver Point, was another spot beloved of the Wordsworths, with pretty cottages and gardens filled with hollyhocks and red-hot pokers. Wainwright fell for

There are no speedboats on Ullswater, just the odd puttering motorboat and classic red-sailed dinghies.

it too, calling the path from Sandwick to nearby Martindale 'the most beautiful and rewarding in lakeland'. To the south, Scalehow Force waterfall tumbles down rocks in a pristine wood. To the north lies the enchanting Howtown Hotel. Set idyllically amid wild-flower meadows, it lures walkers to the tiny, wood-panelled public bar for a cold beer, or tea and scones in the garden. At the southern end of the walk, in Patterdale, hikers stop for tea and ice-cream at Side Farm.

No wonder Dorothy Wordsworth's verdict of a 'perfect summertime walk' remains true two centuries later. Take your Ordnance Survey map, your Kendal mint cake and Alfred Wainwright's *Far Eastern Fells*, and start climbing. It took 'AW' two years to walk and chart the surrounding pikes, crags, fells and tarns for his second pictorial guide, but he reached the same inescapable conclusion that all visitors do, calling Ullswater a place of 'supreme loveliness'.

OTHER BEAUTY SPOTS

The western shore of Ullswater, flanked by the busy A592, is a honeypot on summer weekends. Even so, it is a beguiling journey with fine views across the lake to Hallin Fell and Place Fell. Wordsworth's Point, at Glencoyne Bay, is where the 'host of golden daffodils' reappear each spring. Here, too, is the Lake District's most celebrated waterfall, Aira Force, dropping 70 feet amid Victorian landscaped parkland. Protected red squirrels make occasional appearances around Aira Force or Gowbarrow Fell (there are a series of walks from the National Trust car park).

South of Ullswater is lovely little Brotherswater Tarn and the picturesque village of Hartsop, departure point for scenic walks. Haweswater, east of Hartsop, is home to the last wild golden eagle in England; its mate died in 2005, and as eagles mate for life, it is unlikely to find another partner. You may spot it soaring on its lonely flight over Riggindale Crags from the RSPB bird hide (01931 713376, www.rspb.org.uk), along with buzzards and peregrine falcons.

WHERE TO STAY & EAT

Howtown Hotel (01768 486514, www.howtown-hotel.com) has no email address, no fax machine and they don't take credit cards; there's no television, tea tray or telephone in the rooms. But they don't need them at this timeless retreat, where loyal guests return for Mrs Baldry's antique-filled public rooms and beautiful garden. Pre-dinner drinks are taken on the immaculate lawn or in the plush and intimate red bar, before diners are summoned by gong for a 7pm dinner. Four courses of traditional English fare make no concession to foodie fashion. Coffee is poured from old silverware and beds are turned back at night. It's old fashioned, understated and irresistible.

England's first country house hotel, Sharrow Bay, is arguably the best (01768 486301, www.sharrowbay.co.uk). Opened in 1948, it continues to offer lavish hospitality in an elegant mansion. There are over-the-top public rooms, glamorous bedrooms, magnificent gardens and sensational food. Book ahead for sumptuous afternoon teas and dinners. Try the sticky toffee pudding – it was invented here.

The Quiet Site (07768 727016, www.thequietsite.co.uk) is a well-equipped campsite: the funky timber pods are just the job when you can't be bothered with poles and ropes.

Near Penrith, the George & Dragon (01768 865 381, www.georgeand dragonclifton.co.uk) is a 17th-century coaching inn with contemporary bedrooms and accomplished cooking with an emphasis on local produce. Nearby, Whitbysteads Hill Farm (01931 712284, www.whitbysteads.org) is a characterful old farmhouse B&B in a pretty village, with three bedrooms decorated in an eclectic style and a whiff of faded splendour.

Set in *Withnail & I* country (Uncle Monty's cottage is nearby, the phone box in Bampton), Mardale Inn @ St Patrick's Well (Bampton, 01931 713 244, www.mardale inn.co.uk) is a stylish pub that serves simple, simple, well-cooked dishes of 'tattie pot' (meat and potato stew), Herdwick burger and Morecambe Bay potted shrimps. Dogs welcome; accommodation available.

HOW TO GET THERE

Ullswater is southwest of Penrith and due north of Windermere. **By car** The M6 to Penrith is the nearest motorway. From there, the A592 is a short drive to Ullswater. The B5320 from Penrith goes to Pooley Bridge on the north-eastern tip of the lake. **By train** The nearest station to Ullswater is Penrith (National Rail Enquiries, 08457 484950). **By bus** National Express run coaches to Penrith. Stagecoach buses operate within Cumbria (0871 200 2233, www. stagecoachbus.com). For scenic bus journeys around the lakes, contact the National Park and ask for the Give the Driver a Break leaflets (or download them from the website) (01539 724555, www. lake-district.gov.uk). **By boat** There are cruises of Ullswater departing almost hourly from Pooley Bridge, Glenridding or Howtown (01768 482229, www. ullswater-steamers.co.uk) in the summer, and less frequently during the off-season. **On foot** The footpath described in this book is between Glenridding and Howtown. You can take the Ullswater Steamer for the first leg of the journey or do it in reverse. Scenic footpaths also leave from Martindale, Patterdale, Sandwick and Pooley Bridge. For more walks, see www.ullswater.co.uk or visit Ullswater TIC. **Map** Ordnance Survey Explorer OL5, The English Lake District NE Area; grid ref NY431205.

FURTHER REFERENCE

See Cumbria Tourist Information service (01539 822222, www.golakes.co.uk); Lake District National Park (01539 724555, www.lake-district.gov.uk); Ullswater Tourist Information Centre (main car park, Glenridding, 01768 482414).

Cheviot Hills

In a lonely place.

'In Northumberland alone, both heaven and earth are seen.' So wrote the historian GM Trevelyan, and it's easy to see why: if hell is other people, then vast, empty Northumberland could be the entrance to the pearly gates. The county's 1,936 square miles are the most sparsely populated in England, and less than 2,000 people live within the 405 square miles of the Northumberland National Park. And if that doesn't give you sufficient air to breathe, the Cheviot Hills are the least-visited part of the least-visited national park in England. Lest you think this an exaggeration, on our most recent visit – in mid June at that – the only human being spotted was 100 feet up and travelling at Mach 1 in an RAF fighter plane (he didn't wave back). Is that space enough?

It may be empty, but is that all the Cheviots have to offer? Is there any there there? If adjectives like solitary, windswept and bleak fill you with anticipation, rather than a desire for a Martini and decent reception for your mobile phone, you may have found your earthly paradise. After all, in these crowded islands, a place where you can walk all day and not see another soul is precious indeed.

But the Cheviots has more than just splendid isolation to recommend it. Most travel writers highlight its geology (worn-down volcanoes and built-up silt), archaeological significance (hunters, gatherers, hill forts) and history (the Romans came, looked around and went back behind the Wall), but while all of this is valuable, it's not the best way to convey an idea of the Cheviots. For this is a land of impressions, of cloud shapes cast upon hills of green and brown, and its essence lies in the waving flags of cotton grass, the brief blaze of heather and the fleeting glory of hay meadows. It's a paradox that these huge, vast and smooth hills, with their wide-open vistas, leave only fragmentary images in the memory: tangles of wool dangling from hollowed-out gorse bushes like tattered beards; flowers small and bright as stars speckling the grass.

The hills are demarcated by heather and bracken, plantations and moors, but one of the other lasting impressions of the Cheviots is the drystone walls. These are so much a feature of the environment that it's easy to overlook what an extraordinary exercise in hard labour and applied topology they represent. The illiterate labourers who made them would be worthy of a chair in mathematics at Cambridge University today, such was their ability to add irregular, multi-sided objects together and make a smooth-sided wall.

A sheep stell in Harthope Valley (above); the bleak beauty of Housey Crags (right).

The other great shapers of the landscape are the four-legged, bleating lawn mowers: wherever you go in the Cheviots, sheep speckle the hillsides and add life to the lonely walks. And they're a strange flock: venture up on to Housey Crags on the way to the distinctive round top of Hedgehope, and the large number of droppings suggest that the beasts must have a desire for romantic vistas and breezy landscapes to match the Romantic poets – it can't be the grass, as there is none on these exposed rocks.

Sheep aren't the only ones to frequent the hill tops. Our Iron Age ancestors studded the region with their makeshift wooden dwellings, but it is not clear why they switched to building hill forts around 500BC, or why they constructed them in such high and exposed positions – defence, prestige? – but one thing soon becomes apparent when labouring to the top of Yeavering Bell or Brough Law: they must have had thighs like tree trunks.

That walk to the hill fort on Yeavering Bell in particular produces musings on Shelley's poem 'Ozymandias', about the decline of great men and empires ('Look on my works, ye mighty, and despair'). That's because the climb begins at the site of Ad Gefrin, once the palace of King Edwin, the Northumbrian Warrior King (AD585-633). It's now a field – sheep graze where the chieftain of Yeavering Bell once sat, lord of all he surveyed. But the high, desolate Cheviots help you keep things in perspective. For even a monarch's orders must have sounded feeble when uttered in the heights. Try speaking out loud when you're alone on the hills: your voice will sound like breath blown by the wind: quiet, fleeting, mortal.

Harthope woodland (above) is one of the more bucolic corners of the lonely Cheviots; Upper Coquetdale (below) is typical of the region's smooth, empty hills. Next page: a view across the Barrowburn hay meadow up the Coquet Valley.

Other, different, voices sound more at home here. The hay meadows of Barrowburn are heavy with the buzzing of bumblebees, while the whale-backed ridge of the Cheviot – the singular hill from which the range takes its name – comes alive in summer with the song of the meadow pipit, singing as it labours upwards and then falls, trilling, away, or the skylark, diminishing to a black dot against the clouds, its voice filling the empty, windy wastes with bubbling streams of music. But most of all, the high hills are the range of the ravens. If you're lucky, you might see a pair, riding the rolling air, or hear their extraordinary call, like two pieces of hollow wood being clapped together. The lower reaches are where their more voluble cousins, the rooks and the crows, abide, in gossiping, hurrying flocks, looking rather like the crowd at a Sisters of Mercy gig.

The world has changed a great deal since people first came to the Cheviots. Then the Wild Wood was an encroaching threat on the scattered pockets of humanity; now it's reduced to a few preserved islands in the sea of humanity. The hills stand largely bare in a sombre, grave landscape of muted greens and browns. They don't invite you. They don't even notice you. But should the press of people become too great, the endless procession of anonymous faces too numbing, then come here, stand upon a cloud-flecked hill and hear the voice of the wind. You'll be the only one listening.

OTHER BEAUTY SPOTS

Had enough of hills? Head to the coast. The shores of Northumberland are an Area of Outstanding Natural Beauty and the stretch between Holy Island in the north and Alnmouth in the south is as beautiful and unspoiled a coast as you could hope to find: miles of pristine sandy beaches, barely a soul on them and an entire sea to yourself. All right, it's

the North Sea, which explains the lack of bathers, but stand on the beach at Bamburgh, with the castle looming behind you, Holy Island to your left and Dunstanburgh Castle to your right, and the lighthouses of the Farne Islands winking at you from across the water, and it's hard to think of a more extraordinary shoreline: a double whammy of nature and history, each serving to highlight and complement the other.

WHERE TO STAY & EAT

In Northumberland, B&Bs and holiday cottages account for the vast majority of accommodation, although many pubs offer rooms too. Top-of-the-range hotels are rare, but Chathill's Doxford Hall (01665 589700, www.doxfordhall.com), a luxurious period piece with swimming pool, spa and swish restaurant, is an exception.

Hethpool House B&B (01668 216232, www.hethpoolhouse.co.uk), near Wooler, has a storybook feel, with its Arts-and-Crafts architecture and valley setting in the heart of the Cheviots. Locally sourced meals include roast Cheviots lamb with blueberry jelly and Tweed salmon steaks. Also near Wooler, the Hemmel (01668 283165, www.thehemmel wooler.co.uk) is a down-to-earth choice: the decor is not fashionable, but the lovely valley setting, charming courtyard and friendly owners make up for it.

There are plenty of self-catering cottages nearby, but if you're willing to stay closer to the coast, the Ducket (Outchester, 01668 213336, www.rosscottages.co.uk) is an 18th-century tower that's been buffed and polished to 21st-century standards – a romantic retreat for two. Doxford Cottages (01665 589393, www.doxfordcottages.co.uk) are set on a bucolic, 2,500-acre estate with its own lake; the magnificent castle coast (Dunstanburgh and Bamburgh) is nearby.

In Belford, the B&B at Outchester Manor (01668 213767, www.outchestermanor. co.uk) is a good-looking, grey stone farmhouse with comfortable, homely rooms.

Despite some fine local produce, Northumberland is no foodie destination. The pubs will fill you up with honest but mundane food, but you may go out of your way to find a truly memorable meal. For light lunches, Breeze (Wooler, 01668 283333, www.breeze wooler.com) serves home-made soup, quiches and cappuccinos in an art-gallery setting, while the Ship Inn in Low Newton by the Sea (01665 576262, www.shipinnnewton.co.uk) serves good pub food including fresh fish, vegetarian dishes using locally sourced ingredients and old-fashioned English puddings. For something fancier, you must drive down the A1 to Blackmore's of Alnwick (01665 602395, www.blackmoresofalnwick.com), an elegant boutique-style hotel that serves more upmarket fare.

HOW TO GET THERE

The Cheviot Hills lie in the north of Northumberland, near the Scottish Borders, between Woolder, Jedburgh and Rothbury. **By car** The A697, which branches from the A1 just north of Newcastle, runs up the eastern flank of the Cheviots. Access roads into the National Park run from the A697 (look for signs saying 'Northumberland National Park'). If you want to hire a car locally, a representative of Berwick Car Hire (01289 307611, www.berwickcarhire.co.uk) will meet you off the train at Berwick-upon-Tweed – and be at the station when it's time to leave. **By train** East Coast Mainline to Berwick-upon-Tweed (08457 225225, www.nationalexpresseastcoast. com), then hire car (see above). **By bus** There's no public transport into the Cheviots. National Express has coaches from London to Berwick-upon-Tweed (08717 818181, www.nationalexpress. com). **On foot** For Housey Crag, Hedgehope and The Cheviot, take the road to Earle from Wooler, and then head towards Langleeford. Drive down into the valley, park in a layby and head off. For Yeavering Bell, take the B6351 off the A697 north of Wooler and park in the layby near the site of Ad Gefrin. For the hay meadows at Barrowburn, drive to Alwinton and then take the narrow road into the National Park. There is parking (and a nice tea room) near the meadows. **Map** Ordnance Survey Explorer OL16, the Cheviot Hills; grid ref NT995285.

FURTHER REFERENCE

There are tourist information offices in Alnwick (01665 511333); Berwick-upon-Tweed (01289 330733); Seahouses (01665 720 884); and Wooler (01668 282123). For all, see www.visitnorthumberland.com.

Dinas

A natural remedy.

L ush, soothing and secluded, the Dinas bird sanctuary is also a haven for humans. This secret pocket of Carmarthenshire, in mid-Wales, offers a natural remedy for the stress of modern life. For a start, the background noise resembles the track listing of a relaxation CD: birdsong echoing under a woodland canopy; a gurgling stream; a rushing river; soft rainfall, and wind rustling through the trees. All that's missing is the crashing surf (the thunderous River Towy makes up for it) and the whale sounds (although the occasional baa of a sheep adds a pastoral charm). If Dinas sounds like a wellness CD, it also looks like the cover of one, with misty, soft-focus scenes of verdant deciduous forest – oak, birch, alder and willow – and foaming white waterfalls.

If that sounds too New Age pretty, relief is at hand: the softness is punctuated by rugged outbursts: jagged outcrops, grey shale slopes and austere hills, above which soars the red kite, a majestic bird of prey. In the foothills of the Cambrian mountains, this is where the soft scenery of southern Wales meets the spartan and dramatic north. This clash of landscapes makes for a complex beauty, but the striking contrasts produce a harmonious whole – a bit like the dawn chorus of tits, thrushes, woodpeckers and warblers at this 2,000-acre RSPB sanctuary.

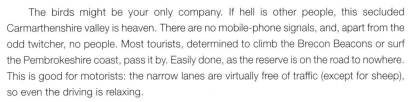

The pied flycatcher is one of the avian stars of this RSPB reserve; the River Towy (below) runs through it.

The birds might be your only company. If hell is other people, this secluded Carmarthenshire valley is heaven. There are no mobile-phone signals, and, apart from the odd twitcher, no people. Most tourists, determined to climb the Brecon Beacons or surf the Pembrokeshire coast, pass it by. Easily done, as the reserve is on the road to nowhere. This is good for motorists: the narrow lanes are virtually free of traffic (except for sheep), so even the driving is relaxing.

The Dinas reserve may restore the human spirit, but it was established to save the birds; indeed, it rescued the red kite from the brink of extinction. This iconic bird of prey – known for its forked tail, red plumage and six-foot wingspan – has been around for 120,000 years, soaring acrobatically on thermals. During medieval times, British skies were thick with the scavengers, but as farming expanded, a Vermin Act was passed in 1566 – and a bounty placed on the red kite's head. By 1977, the kite was almost extinct in Britain. The Dinas RSPB Reserve, established in the mid 1970s, became ground zero for Operation Red Kite – Gurkhas were even drafted to guard the eggs from collectors — and a successful comeback was launched (there are now four breeding pairs in the reserve, and 1,200 pairs throughout the UK).

These days, birdwatchers are blasé about red kites, as sightings are common, especially on weekends when local farmers stage feeding shows. The new stars are pied flycatchers, wood warblers and redstarts, rare spring migrants that summer in Welsh oak forests before retiring to Africa for the winter. The pied flycatcher is a dapper little bird – clad in tuxedo-like black and white plumage – with a melodious song. The wood warbler darts about quickly (bring your binoculars to catch a glimpse of its lemon yellow breast), but its song – characterised as 'shimmering and cascading' by RSPB ranger David Anning – is easy to discern. The redstart, a cousin of the robin, is shy, but its quivering red and orange tail is positively flamboyant.

Dinas' fan club is not restricted to birdwatchers: scientists and botanists swoon before its tongue-twisting set of natural credentials: SSSI (Site of Special Scientific Interest), SAC (Special Area of Conservation) and SPA (Special Protection Area). The accolades are partly due to all the velvety moss, delicate ferns and layers of lichen. These fecund carpets cover twisted oak branches and Stone Age boulders, and sustain a who's-who of rare bugs and butterflies (such as the silver-washed fritillary). This supernatural greenery is the result of fresh mountain air and moist conditions. Climatologists say Dinas is Britain's version of a 'cloud forest' – subtropical mountain woodlands found in South America. Cloud forests are also known as fog forests, a more fitting name for Dinas, the dampest corner of Europe (bring an anorak). Still, the gauzy air lends a mystical feel.

So do the rocks. After you leave the boardwalk near the entrance, the gentle forest path gives way to a jagged world of shale, slate, limestone and sandstone, with some clambering required. There are so many rugged boulders strewn among the cold black waters it looks like a quarry exploded. In places, the scene even evokes the American West – more 'Rocky Mountain High' than *How Green Was My Valley*. In fact, this geological display is part of Carmarthenshire culture: quarries were once common in these parts; there's a gold mine nearby in Dolaucothi; and high above Dinas, along a dangerous rocky path, lies a cave where Twm Shon Catti, the Welsh Robin Hood, used to hide out in the 16th century.

For peace of mind, stay close to the river. Its roar drowns out the birdsong, but it also drowns out your cares. With all the rocks, foam and pure water, it's as if you have stumbled into a bottled-water advert. In fact, in Victorian times, Welsh doctors sent their patients to the springs of nearby Llanwrtyd Wells, to take the waters and walk the hills. Solace can also be found away from the water, where wilderness gives way to wistfulness in the form of a bluebell wood: here, warblers sing and sheep graze. It's a fittingly peaceful finale to the walk. For stressed-out souls, Dinas is truly a natural remedy.

The rushing river drowns out the birdsong in places, but its thunderous roar is just as soothing.

OTHER BEAUTY SPOTS

Dinas RSPB lies at the top of the Towy (Tywi) Valley, whose lush, undulating and farm-dotted hills stretch from Carmarthen to Llandovery. The Industrial Revolution passed this valley by: there were no coal mines here, and life on many of these farms hasn't changed

much in a century. Indeed, the medieval legends of Merlin the Magician – Carmarthen's most famous son – live on here. And the River Towy, which winds through the Dinas Reserve, is still overflowing with salmon and sea trout.

Llyn Briane, just north of Dinas, is a dramatic reservoir fringed by coniferous forest plantations. The road follows its shores with photo ops at every bend, before reaching Soar y Mynydd, a lonely 1820 Methodist chapel. A traditional red phone box amid green hills is another postcard shot, reached via a five-minute drive north towards Tregaron. Cwm Rhaeadr, south of Dinas, is another stress-beating reserve that has woodland, warblers and the highest waterfall in the Towy Valley.

Dinefwr Castle, a 12th-century ruin owned by the National Trust, was immortalised by Turner in a 1795 painting; on the edge of the River Towy near Llandeilo, it affords classic valley views. Carregcennen is another romantic ruin near Llandeilo with a sweeping panorama. The magical lake of Llyn y Fan Fach (*see p194*) is also nearby.

The Heart of Wales railway, a charming, one-carriage train, travels from Swansea to Shrewsbury, taking in the ravishing scenery of the Towy Valley and the Brecon Beacons along its 121-mile, four-hour journey.

WHERE TO STAY & EAT

The New White Lion (01550 720685, www.newwhitelion.co.uk) is a tasteful B&B in the grey market town of Llandovery. The six bedrooms are full of luxurious textures – sheepskin rugs, faux animal-skin bedspreads, plush white duvets – and fixtures (rainforest showerheads). The honesty bar in the drawing room adds a touch of boutique hotel. For supper, the dining room (open to residents only) serves country comfort food using local ingredients.

The Cawdor (01558 823500, www.thecawdor.com), in Llandeilo, is a big boutique B&B, with 23 rooms and a modern-classic schtick: period details, bold decor and creature comforts. The elegant restaurant uses local ingredients prepared with flair.

Fronlas (01558 824733, www.fronlas.com), a three-room B&B, has got it all: swish designer decor, a gorgeous location (also in Llandeilo, with views of the hills) and eco credentials (it is solar-powered, and breakfasts are organic).

The Plough Inn (01558 823431, www.ploughrhosmaen.com), on the side of a dual carriageway near Llandeilo, resembles a Travelodge gone posh. The rooms are stylish and well-equipped (pillowtop mattresses, flatscreen TVs, wireless internet) with bucolic views. The bustling restaurant, a local favourite, has gastropub aspirations.

Llanerchindda Farm (01550 750274, www.cambrianway.com) is a cheap alternative to a boutique hotel. Frequented by outdoorsy types who like off-roading in their 4X4s, clay-pigeon shooting and fly fishing, it is set in 50 scenic acres; just don't expect luxury.

Dinas' myriad mosses, lichens and ferns enthrall botanists, and its dramatic rocks lure geologists.

HOW TO GET THERE

The Dinas RSPB is a 2.5-hour drive north of Swansea in Carmarthenshire, 10 miles north of Llandovery on the minor road to Llyn Brianne. **By car** From Swansea, take the M4 and then the A483 through Llandeilo. From Llandovery, follow the signs to Cilycwm, then carry on through the village until you reach the Cross Inn. Turn right, cross the bridge, and then turn left towards Ystradffin. There is a car park on your left before you get to Llyn Brianne. **By train** The Heart of Wales railway stops four times a day in Llandovery (01597 822053, www.heart-of-wales.co.uk), but you really need a car to get to the reserve. **On foot** The Dinas nature reserve has a circular 70-minute walk. The first section is a boardwalk, but the rest of the trail is more rugged; sturdy shoes recommended. **Map** Ordnance Survey Explorer 187, Llandovery; grid ref SN782467.

FURTHER REFERENCE

Llandovery Tourist Office (01550 720693, www.breconbeacons.org). RSPB (01654 700222, www.rspb.org). See also www.enchantedtowy.co.uk.

Llyn y Fan Fach

Magic mountains and legendary lakes.

Anyone who has ever driven across the Alps will be familiar with the sense of vertigo they can induce: narrow, winding roads with terrifying drops to the valley floor thousands of feet below you. There's a place in Wales, however, where your vertigo can be cured. Just take a seat on a rocky outcrop of the Black Mountain in the Brecon Beacons, legs dangling over the ridge that drops 1,300 feet. Strangely, although the sensation is thrilling, it's not frightening. That may be because you are gazing down at Llyn y Fan Fach, a lake synonymous with magic spells. Gazing out across the landscape from such a perch is like taking a funfair ride in widescreen technicolour. Instead of being scared, one falls into a trance.

The mystical nature of the area is well-documented, and with good reason. The stark peaks and ridges and the bleak bare troughs of the Black Mountain conjure up images of otherworldy landscapes laden with foreboding and darkness. The vista from above the lake calls to mind the *The Lord of the Rings*, and Frodo's journey from the gentle shire to the wild mountains of Mordor. There's no known link, but Tolkien did speak Welsh, was influenced by the half-Welsh priest Francis Morgain, and often walked in the area – nearby Ystradfellte, with its waterfalls, limestone and caves, has been suggested as a model for Middle Earth.

If the Brecons did influence Tolkien's epic story of elves and wizards, giants and dwarfs, it would join a series of myths and legends associated with the area: treasure-hoarding serpents, fair maidens turned into silver fish, spring water with special powers. The most famous story about Llyn y Fan Fach is a fairy tale with a touch of kitchen sink: it pairs a creature from a bottomless black lake with a parable about wife-beating. In 'the Lady of the Lake', which supposedly took place in the 12th century, a young farmer is enchanted by a fairy living in Llyn y Fan Fach and woos her. She agrees to become his wife, as long as he heeds her warning: hit me three times and I'll take myself, and our cattle, back to the lake with me forever. Sure enough, over the years, he strikes her three times, and she duly returns to her lake. But she comes back once, to teach her sons healing powers. Later, they become the famous Physicians of Myddfai, a clan of medieval Welsh doctors who, in real life, were renowned for their advanced medical treatments.

Geology has also worked magic here. The lake's magnificently shaped landscape formed during the Ice Age, when glacial waters carved the dramatic clefts and ridges, and the bowl-shaped lake and cirque. The combination of colours is gorgeous, from the red sandstone outcrops to the plush green hillsides.

The lake casts its spell long before it actually comes into view. A gurgling stream, tumbling down in a rocky cascade, accompanies the ascending path from the car park. Inquisitive sheep watch walkers impassively from the fells, but otherwise nothing seems to move. The air is still and silent, apart from the sound of walkers' laboured breathing. A small dam provides a taster for the main event, Llyn y Fan Fach, which lies halfway up the mountain. At first glance, the lake doesn't seem pretty enough for all the fairy-tale stuff. Instead of a vast surface of silvery blue, the water is muddy brown. But stop and stare, and the aura becomes apparent. The lake is framed by vertiginous, velvety green mountains, their rectangular shape echoing Cape Town's Table Mountain. And they are pockmarked with patches of rusty red soil and intriguing striped textures. The panorama is entrancing; the stillness of the waters soothing.

But the major impact is felt above the lake, at the 2,000-foot Bannau Sir Gaer Ridge, another hour up the path. From here, the cirque's folds, jagged rents and criss-crossing

Waterfalls tumble down the mountain on the walk up to Llyn y Fan Fach (next page), site of the legendary lady of the lake.

sheep paths suggest a giant's playground of slides and jumping stones; the sandstone outcrops are there for sitting on (good for a breather) and gazing (the view is spellbinding).

As befits a mystical lake, Llyn y Fan Fach has a twin, Llyn y Fan Fawr. And as befits a legend, you have to make an epic journey to see it: from Bannau Sir Gaer, the steep path continues along the ridge for miles, culminating at the 2,631-foot summit of Bannau Brecheiniog (Brecon Fan), from where there are tremendous views of Llyn y Fan Fawr. Like its twin, the expanse of glittering water hundreds of feet below enchants and draws you in – a Welsh answer to an Alpine odyssey. And once again, any sense of vertigo is cured by the vista – and the special powers of the Lady of the Lake.

OTHER BEAUTY SPOTS

In the Brecon Beacons, beauty spots pop up round every bucolic bend. The Dan yr Ogof Showcaves (01639 730284, www.showcaves.co.uk) are oversold, but eerie and atmospheric once you get inside and away from the crowds.

The Cwm Rhaeadr forest (www.cilycwm.com), north of Llandovery, has a two-mile woodland trail through coniferous forest, with views of the Nant y Rhaeadr waterfalls. This is birdwatching territory, but the best in show is next door at the Dinas RSPB reserve (see p186), a mix of rivers, greenery and pied flycatchers. Llyn Brianne Reservoir, further north, is a man-made slice of beauty fringed by spruce, larch and firs, with photo ops galore.

Wales is famous for its waterfalls, and the cataracts at Pontneddfechan, in the southern part of the Black Mountain, offer close-up views: people actually swim in exhilarating plunge pools along the Neddfechan and Melte rivers. South Wales's highest falls, Henrhyd, are five miles west of here near the village of Coelbren.

Brecon Beacons Mountain Railway (01685 722988, www.breconmountain railway.co.uk) is a quaint steam train that chugs up and down the beauty spots.

WHERE TO STAY & EAT

While Llyn y Fan Fach sits in splendid isolation, good food and accommodation is surprisingly close by. In Llandovery, the smart New White Lion B&B (01550 720685, www.newwhitelion.co.uk) has tasteful decor (including a pale blue and silver Lady of the

Lake room), exemplary country cooking by Sylvia Pritchard and an invaluable guide in the form of her husband, Gerald, who maps out excursions for guests. In Llandeilo, the Georgian, Grade II-listed Cawdor (0800 988 3002, www.thecawdor.com), a 23-room boutique hotel, has laid-back charm and a simple, elegant restaurant.

Llandeilo is also home to the smaller, but equally good, Fronlas (01558 824733, www.fronlas.com), a pretty Edwardian townhouse that is now an eco-friendly guesthouse, with three fashionable and flamboyant rooms. Twenty miles away, at the Felin Fach Griffin (01874 620111, www.eatdrinksleep.ltd.uk), the seven bedrooms are stylishly unfussy, as is the menu – 'simple things done well' – in its acclaimed pub and restaurant.

HOW TO GET THERE

Llyn y Fan Fach lies below the Black Mountain in Carmarthenshire on the edge of the Brecon Beacons. **By road** The starting point for Llyn y Fan Fach is easily reached from Llandovery or Llandeilo on the A4069. Follow signs to the village of Llanddeusant, seven miles south of Llandovery and 12 miles east of Llandeilo. At Llanddeusant, head east along the minor road, following signs to Lady of the Lake (Llyn y Fan Fach). At the farmhouse at the end of the road turn right and follow the road to the car park. **By train** Trains run from Swansea and Shrewsbury to Llandovery and Llandeilo (01554 820586, www.heart-of-wales.co.uk). **By bus** The nearest service is postbus 291 to Myddfai – see Traveline Cymru (0871 2002233, www.traveline-cymru.info) or the Carmarthenshire county website at www.sirgaerfyrddin.gov.uk. **On foot** From the car park east of Llanddeusant, follow the path up the hill; Llyn y Fan Fach is about an hour away. Another hour takes you to the Bannau Sir Gaer Ridge, with a view down to the lake. Follow the trail along the ridge, heading east, for another two hours for a view of Llyn y Fan Fawr, the twin lake. Check weather forecasts as wind can be fierce. Llyn y Fan Fawr can be reached by a 1.2-mile walk across moors from the minor road between Trecastle and Glyntawe. **Map** Ordnance Survey Explorer OL12, Brecon Beacons National Park; grid ref SN802218.

FURTHER REFERENCE

Llandovery Tourist Information Centre (01550 720693, www.visitbrecon beacons.com). See also www.fforest fawrgeopark.org.uk and www.travelbreconbeacons.info

Beddgelert

A watery wonderland.

The wild tumble of the river, the plumpness of the rowan berries and the velvety green of the wooded valley slopes recently earned a Snowdonian gorge the top slot in a beauty competition. Beddgelert, the pretty-as-paint Gwynnedd village, is the gateway to the Pass of Aberglaslyn, current holder of the National Trust's Finest View in Britain award. And it was all down to prodigious rainfall – complaining about the blessed rain in Snowdonia would therefore be as illogical as deploring Arizona sunshine. The village, for instance, is at its most gorgeous after downpours, when the river is in spate. The clouds part and sunlight bounces off rain-washed slate and sparkles on the boiling torrent, which rushes under an ivy-clad stone bridge.

Beddgelert stands where two rivers flow down Mount Snowdon's flanks on their way to the sea. The rivers, Afon Glaslyn and Nant Colwyn, meet in the village in a glorious rush of water that alternately thrills or frightens local canoeists. After it has rained hard, the trees at the water's edge are partly submerged and the grassland all marshy. Walkers setting off to see Beddgelert's claim to fame – a slaughtered wolfhound's final resting place – need waterproof boots.

Said wolfhound, Gelert, has spawned a great shaggy dog story. The faithful pet of Llywelyn the Great, a 12th-century prince, Gelert was mistakenly slaughtered by his master after being suspected of trying to kill his son and heir; it turned out the dog had saved the boy's life. So filled with remorse was the prince, he supposedly erected a memorial stone to his pet near the river, and the name of the village was born ('grave of Gelert'). In fact, the grave was put there by a 19th-century innkeeper trying to lure tourists – those Victorians loved a mawkish tear-jerker. Two centuries later, visitors still beat a path to the grave, unaware that the village actually got its name from St Celer, an eighth-century monk who settled here. It didn't boom until the 19th century, when the slate industry took off and the rise of the Great British Holiday prompted an upsurge in Snowdonian travel (would-be Grand Tourists were forced to stay in Britain during the Napoleonic wars).

Today, the rocky buildings of Beddgelert, a winner of the Britain in Bloom competition, are garlanded with flowers. Every handsome stone dwelling sports window boxes and pots spilling over with petunias and lobelia. But Beddgelert is just a warm-up for an even more head-turning beauty spot: the aforementioned Pass of Aberglaslyn, a rocky gorge hewn by the fast-flowing river, and easily reached from the village along a riverside path. Described in 1862 by George Borrow, the author of *Wild Wales*, as 'a wondrous valley, rivalling for grandeur and beauty any vale either in the Alps or Pyrenees', Aberglaslyn is one of the most photographed places in the country. With its ever-changing moods – from craggy, lofty drama and turbulent waters, to leafy, sun-dappled winsomeness – it is a true Welsh pin-up. The steep hillsides – thick with bracken, boulders and mossy trees – are awe-inspiring. Sometimes the path disappears under the foaming river, forcing you to remove boots and socks and paddle along.

Plants that don't mind getting their feet wet do well here. The exuberance of the river creates a springy, boggy habitat that supports hardy blooms, such as ling heather, which makes the valley blush pinkly in spring and summer. Starry flowers of lady's mantle (*alchemilla*) dot the rocks by the streams. In the steep woodlands, bluebells create a wash of colour and in the flood plains below, the grass is spattered with buttercups and pale lilac lady's smock (Mayflower). On summer days, walkers toiling up the slope of Cwm Bychan can refresh themselves with wild blueberries that grow among the heather.

Unfamiliar bird calls turn your attention from the flora. You may see a pair of choughs chatting: although you're more likely to see ravens, the chough's shiny black plumage and blood-red beak and legs help it stand out. Red kites also hunt high above the bracken. The feathered celebrities of Aberglaslyn, however, are the ospreys. For five summers, a pair have flown in from Africa to raise chicks in the Glaslyn Valley. They even have their own reality television show – a live nestcam sends pictures of the birds to television screens

The prodigious rainfall and abundance of rivers and lakes create a boggy, springy habitat in and around Beddgelert.

at an RSPB hide at Pont Creosor. Visitors also use binoculars to watch the ospreys plummeting into the water and emerging with a fish in their claws.

An uneasy balance between tourism and nature conservation dogs the area. The opening of the Welsh Highland Railway's new steam line to Beddgelert has ruffled feathers among conservationists. But train enthusiasts point out that when the river is tempestuous, the safest way see the Pass of Aberglaslyn is from a railway carriage.

The plentiful water supply that nourishes the landscape has also encouraged a more insidious ornamentation. Rhododendron *ponticum*, with its showy carmine flowers, is a fatal beauty. Thriving in the damp conditions and acid soil, this alien is barging across the valley, blocking out the light with its thick, leathery leaves. Other plant species can't compete and die off, starving the insects and birds. Victorian gardeners unwittingly created the problem by introducing the species; now environmentalists are slashing and burning. The short-term results may look alarming, but no pain, no gain: every great beauty must yield to a little cosmetic assistance at some stage in her lifetime.

Beddgelert village is known for its stone bridge, rushing rivers, floral displays and the grave of Gelert; a tourist train (right) takes in the scenic splendour of the Pass of Aberglaslyn.

OTHER BEAUTY SPOTS

Hafod Garreg, a low-lying wetland south of Beddgelert near Nantmor, is a small nature reserve where craggy mountain scenery gives way to boggy river walks. Here, Atlantic sessile oaks are interspersed with whispering birches and rowan, with an underlayer of hazel and holly. On the ground, bog grasses such as sheep's fescue, bog myrtle and white-beak sedge create a pretty carpet. Moss and lichens cling attractively to the trees.

Moel Hebog (Hill of the Falcon) breathes down Beddgelert's neck and challenges walkers to put down their gift-shop fudge and trudge. This mountain (2,500 feet) might not have the glamour of its loftier neighbours, and the tricky terrain mixes bog and scree, but it offers splendid isolation from trippers. The steep scramble to the summit affords glorious views of Snowdon; you can then walk along Natlle Ridge to scale other peaks.

The dark surface of Llyn Dinas is graced by reflections of the clouded hills – a classic Snowdonia calendar shot. These still waters do not run so deep – 32 feet at most – but they're laced with mystery: the ubiquitous Merlin the magician apparently unleashed the Red Dragon, the sacred symbol of Wales, from Dinas Emrys, a nearby hill fort.

WHERE TO STAY & EAT

Plas Tan y Graig (01766 890310, www.plas-tanygraig.co.uk) overlooks the Glaslyn river and has inspirational views of Moel Hebog. It's a B&B in a roomy Victorian house, run in friendly fashion by Sharon and Tony, who dispense walking advice and packed lunches. The seven en suite rooms are spacious, plainly appointed and quiet. With a cool beer in your hand, the pretty terrace is heavenly on a sunny evening.

The enormous Royal Goat Hotel (01766 890224, www.royalgoathotel.co.uk) presides over the village like an old colonel who's seen better days. It has a faded grandeur, with heavy dark furniture that smells of beeswax. Its dining room (open to non-residents) is renowned for formal, but good-value, slap-up dinners. Dogs allowed.

Sygun Fawr Country House (01766 890258, www.sygunfawr.co.uk) is a grand 17th-century mansion with a rhododendron-fringed garden and fine views of the valley. The decor is a tad flouncy, but comfortable, and there are creaky floors and rustic beams. The four-course dinner is strong on local lamb and Welsh cheeses (non-residents book ahead).

Tanronen Inn (01766 890347, www.tanronnen.co.uk), a favourite with Beddgelert regulars, goes to town on its floral displays. It has comfortable rooms and reasonable rates, a packed lunch service and a warm fire in the bar. The simple restaurant serves minted Welsh lamb with seasonal vegetables and local salmon or trout from the river.

The nearest youth hostel is the 73-bedder YHA Bryn Gwynant Nant Gwynant (0845 371 9108, www.yha.org.uk), a lovely old manor house near the shores of Llyn Gwynant.

The antique-filled Beddgelert Bistro (01766 890543, www.beddgelert-bistro.co.uk) serves Welsh lamb, Anglesey seafood, wild boar and goose in an old stone building.

The countryside around Beddgelert is dotted with waterfalls, particularly around Llyn Gwynant.

HOW TO GET THERE

Beddgelert lies in North Wales seven miles north of Porthmadog and 12 miles south of Caernarfon. The path to Gelert's grave and the pass of Aberglaslyn is clearly signposted from the village. **By road** Beddgelert is on the junction of the A4085 and the A498. **By train** Nearest station Porthmadog (08456 061660, www.arrivatrainswales.co.uk). Beddgelert is served by trains on the narrow-gauge Welsh Highland Railway from Caernarfon and Porthmadog (01766 516000). **By bus** Beddgelert is served by Bus Gwynedd nos. 97, 98 and Snowdon Sherpa nos. S4, S97 (08712 002233, www.gwynedd.gov.uk). **On foot** The walk through the Pass of Aberglaslyn over Cwym Bychan and round to Llyn Dinas starts at Beddgelert village and is clearly signposted. A popular route up Snowdon starts at the car park at Rhyd-Ddu. Paths leading to lakes Llyn Gwynant and Llyn Dinas are signposted from the A498. **By bicycle** Beddgelert Bikes (01766 890434, www.beddgelertbikes.co.uk) is by the Beddgelert Forest campsite on the A4085. **Map** Ordnance Survey Explorer OL17, Snowdon; grid ref SH589481.

FURTHER REFERENCE

Beddgelert Tourism Association (01766 890312, www.beddgelerttourism.com). Snowdonia National Park (01766 890615, www.eryri-npa.gov.uk).

Loch Etive

A fjord fiesta.

Loch Etive could easily be renamed Loch Mendacious. Consider the dissembling that goes on here. By geological happenstance, Loch Etive is not a lake at all, but a sea loch: Scotland's answer to a Norwegian fjord, it contains salt water and has a very narrow outlet to the sea at Connel. This gives rise to the tidal Falls of Lora, which are more a patch of white water than an obvious Niagara (indeed, because they are tidal, sometimes they do not flow at all). What is more, Loch Etive almost gives you two lochs for the price of one: the lake is physically divided into upper and lower, by narrows between Taynuilt and Bonawe. The name, too, is deceptive: Loch Etive is thought to mean 'little ugly one' in Gaelic, but the scenery, particularly on the remote upper loch, is sublime. Finally, the loch's wild beauty belies its industrial history: the landscape is dotted with fish farms, old iron works, jetties and quarries. Many visitors would rather ignore these dirty little secrets and be swept away by the majestic views.

The landscape is suitably imposing – the skyline is framed by peaks that rise to over 3,000 feet – and wildlife adds to the glory. There is a common seal colony on the upper loch by Inverliver Bay; ospreys and sea eagles fly; and there are deer on the hillsides. Such big country is conducive to big ideas: little wonder an order of monks called the Valliscaulians set up shop at Ardchattan, on the north shore, in around 1230 (originating in Burgundy, they later merged with the Cistercians before dissolving after the Reformation). Although the monks were a particularly austere order, Ardchattan radiates atmosphere: behind the dour, stone priory, there is a ruined chapel and romantic, rose-strewn gardens overlooking the loch. But the story of Loch Etive goes even further back, from the realms of history into Celtic folklore: Deirdre of the Sorrows, the tragic heroine of Irish mythology, fled Ireland with her lover, Naoise, to escape an arranged marriage to the King of Ulster, Conchobar Mac Nessa. The exiled couple lived in bliss on the shores of Loch Etive, until the King had Naoise killed, and Deirdre died of a broken heart.

Mountains, monks and myth – put it all together and Loch Etive melds beauty, nature, romance, spirituality, tragedy and wilderness. You can feel this exceptional quality in your soul, especially on the isolated upper reaches of the loch. And yet all is not pristine. Take Bonawe, for example. Between the village of Taynuilt and the shore lie the ruins of the Bonawe Iron Furnace, built in 1753. Given the plentiful supply of local trees for charcoal, it made sense to ship iron ore to a site where it could be smelted in situ. Tens of thousands of cannonballs for the Napoleonic Wars were made here, and the furnace operated for 120 years. Does it look like a bleak, dystopian ruin, however? No, it looks like a collection of quaint, tumbledown mill buildings, nicely maintained by Historic Scotland, almost as if they had grown from the ground in their mesopotamian setting.

On the opposite shore of the loch, just east of the narrows, you can also see Bonawe Quarries, where hundreds of thousands of tonnes of granite have been stripped from the hillside. Viewed on boat trips run by Loch Etive Cruises, the quarrying looks like a wound in the earth, but the damage occupies a tiny proportion of this giant's landscape; less intrusive fish farms at the loch are virtually invisible by comparison. Head out on the boat from Kelly's Pier and, yes, man's handiwork will be briefly obvious, but your eyes soon go to mountains like Ben Cruachan (3,695 feet) or Ben Starav (3,537 feet). The peaks lend a dominant scale that makes our efforts to dent the natural world appear almost trivial.

At the very head of the loch, towards the obvious cone of Stob Dubh (3,142 feet), there is more evidence of human intervention with the ruins of a boathouse and jetty where, during the Victorian era, a steamer from Oban used to collect and deposit passengers; the connecting minor road shambles on to Glen Coe.

So what to make of the gritty underbelly to all the gorgeousness? It is easy to be seduced by the romance of the Ulster myths, medieval priories and whispering antique hills, while ignoring the charcoal supplies, granite quarries and trout farms. Most travellers come to Scotland for fresh air and virgin scenery. But if we fail to notice economic activity, opting to see another narrative in the landscapes and wildlife, then we're lying to ourselves. Virtually no part of the British Isles remains utterly untouched by civilisation and progress. Loch Etive lays this anomaly bare, betraying the roots of modern industry amid the splendour. You can choose to see nature unadorned, fibbing to yourself about the loch's purity, but why not tell the truth? Even if you take centuries of human intervention

into account, Loch Etive remains magnificent: accessible and beautiful, ancient and modern, alive, but with an echo of Scottish and Irish ghosts. Loch Mendacious? If anything, Loch Etive should be nicknamed Loch Verity.

Cone-shaped mountains characterise the wild and mysterious upper loch.

OTHER BEAUTY SPOTS

For more big dramatic hills and big country, Glen Coe is an obvious destination, famed for its archetypal Highland scenes and bloody history (the notorious MacDonald massacre of 1692). If you approach it from the east, via Bridge of Orchy and the A82, the ideal mountain shape of the Buachaille Etive Mor looms above the moor. Its classic vista is a far cry from the twisted, towering landscape to come when you enter the glen proper.

The imposing Loch Awe, south of Loch Etive, is perfectly named: it's the longest freshwater loch in Scotland (25 miles); it is dotted with castles (including the photogenic ruin of Kilchurn), and it's dominated by the high peak of Ben Cruachan (3,697 feet).

Oban is the departure point for ferries to a host of islands, but principally Mull, one of the largest and best-loved of the Hebrides. For all ferry details, see www.calmac.co.uk.

WHERE TO STAY & EAT

For accommodation, Dun na Mara is a boutique guesthouse (01631 720233, www. dunnamara.com) with views of Mull; it's in Benderloch, north of Oban. South of Oban, you can walk to the coast from stylish Lerags House (01631 563381, www.leragshouse.com) or bird watch in the gardens. For grander things, try Ardanaiseig Hotel (01866 833333, www.ardanaiseig.com), a Victorian pile on Loch Awe. The upmarket Isle of Eriska Hotel & Spa (01631 720371, www.eriskahotel.co.uk) is a baronial manor on an island at Loch Creran. The smart Airds Hotel, by Loch Linnhe, (01631 730236, www.airds-hotel.com) has softly decorated, elegant rooms and its restaurant has one of the best chefs in Argyll.

Nearby Oban is full of restaurants. For fresh fish with water views, Temple Seafood (01631 566000, www.templeseafood.co.uk) is superb, but only open four evenings a week. Seafood is also the forte at Ee-Usk (01631 565666, www.eeusk.com): choose from local mussels and oysters, say, or wild halibut, or smoked salmon from Inverawe. Stylish, rustic Cuan Mor (01631 565078, www.cuanmor.co.uk) has a casual bar-bistro feel and uses local ingredients; Coast (01631 569900, www.coastoban.com) has a chic feel and menu (Oban crab salad with crème fraîche, Aberdeen angus steak with red wine jus).

For pubs, the Clachaig Inn (01855 811252, www.clachaig.com) at Glen Coe is a local legend beloved of climbers and tourists; it also has rooms. The Inverawe Smokehouses (08448 475490), near Taynuilt, has a tea room and sells smoked salmon from its shop.

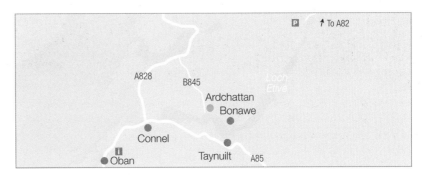

HOW TO GET THERE

Loch Etive is a sea loch in Argyll on the west coast of Scotland, 75 miles north of Glasgow. **By road** The nearest town is Oban. From Glasgow take the A82, then the A85, which goes through both Taynuilt and Connel on the southern reaches of the lower Loch Etive. The loch is also easily accessible by road on the north shore. For the scenic head of the upper loch, stay on the A82 from Glasgow, via Crianlarich, towards Glen Coe: a mile after the sign for Kingshouse Hotel, turn left on the minor road down Glen Etive. Note: this is a dead-end. Most of upper Loch Etive is inaccessible by car; to see it, you must take a boat trip, or walk. **By train** The train to Oban stops at both Taynuilt and Connel Ferry (three trains a day from Glasgow Queen Street, National Rail Enquiries, 08457 484950). **By bus** Scottish Citylink runs the coach service from Glasgow Buchanan Street station to Oban, also stopping at Taynuilt and Connel (08705 50 50 50, www.city link.co.uk).**By boat** Loch Etive Cruises (07721 732703 daytimes, 01866 822430 evenings, www.homeatfirst.com/loch) leave from Kelly's Pier near Taynuilt. Trips run from mid March to late November. Trips out of season by arrangement. **On foot** The Inverawe Smokehouses, east of Taynuilt, has trails to the track by the upper loch. Or turn off the A82 at the sign for Glen Etive, drive to loch, park by old pier and follow the lochside path (six miles return). There are walks from Bonawe (see http://walking.visitscotland.com). **Map** Ordnance Survey Explorer 376, Oban & North Lorn; grid ref NN005335.

FURTHER REFERENCE

The nearest tourist information centre is in Oban (Argyll Square, 01631 563122, www.visitscotland.com). There is also a visitor centre at Inverawe Smokehouses (08448 475490).

Loch Rannoch

Wild at heart.

Britain's last wolf was hunted down, and shot, somewhere in Scotland a few hundred years ago. Several locations lay claim to this dubious distinction, among them Loch Arkaig, in Lochaber, in 1680; or Findhorn, in Moray, in 1743. But the most recent contender (1747) is a place called Mullinavadie (mill of the wolf), on the hillside above the eastern end of Perthshire's Loch Rannoch. And this kill was not the outcome of an epic hunt, involving cunning and skill and exquisite weaponry; instead, the miller's wife, defending her child, ended the wolf's life with a spurtle – a large wooden porridge stirrer. Quite how she did it is not recorded, but evidently this particular wolf was no match for the fierce courage of a protective mother.

Of course, this could be just another death-by-spurtle story in a land which is brimful of legend, but anyone venturing up this archetypal highland glen – loch cupped in forest and mountain – from Pitlochry to Loch Rannoch will be able to picture wolves here, as this majestic landscape has changed little in the last few hundred years. And there's a simple reason for this immutability; the Rannoch glen is a long dead end. It's not on the way to anywhere else – unless you're a wolf or a deer – so anybody who goes up the road in a car, has to come down it again. And many of those who do bother to make the 18-mile journey along the shores of Loch Rannoch to Rannoch Moor don't quite know what to make of what they find there.

Scotland

After twisting and turning through boulder-strewn heath, the B846 finally evaporates at Rannoch Station. Here the skies are huge, the expanse of blanket mire is vast, the weather is forbidding, and the handful of people wandering around are looking rather dazed and perplexed. Certainly the 56-square-mile moor, which until 10,000 years ago hosted Britain's very last glacier, is a godforsaken place to end up for anyone who doesn't believe in the spiritually refreshing power of raw and elemental nature. It's definitely wolf territory.

Rannoch's visitors arrive here in one of two ways. Either up the road along the loch side, or along the only man-made transport link that dares to cross the moor: the Glasgow to Fort William railway. Thanks to this railway, which itself was a legend in the laying (blanket mire's main constituent, sphagnum moss, can hold up to eight times its own weight in water), Rannoch has a daily smog-to-bog sleeper train from London. The train is a kind of Tardis of the railway industry: you step in among lattes and taxis, and step out among deer and midges.

Once upon a time Rannoch was, of course, a considerably more populous place, both in terms of people and wolves. The shores of Loch Rannoch were surrounded in clan settlements, with Stewarts, MacGregors, Menzies, MacDonalds, Robertsons, Camerons and MacDougalls, all with a presence here. Today there's little reminder of their passing, other than the gatherings of stout-trunked Caledonian pines, standing on the hillsides like solitary old chieftains, who only stiffly acknowledge the wind. Hardly anyone lives here now.

And the pines, too, are nearly extinct. Together, they make up one of the last fragments of ancient pine forest, the Black Wood of Rannoch, on the loch's southern shore; it is reached via a pathway (take the one flagged with yellow markers) up from Carie. Much of Scotland was once swathed in such woodland, and Rannoch Moor is littered with skeletal stumps and root systems that have been preserved in the peat for hundreds

A rugged mountain stream at the head of the loch (left); the vista from Queen's View (above).

of years. But this Great Wood of Caledonia was cut and burned by man, partly for fuel, partly for timber, and partly because of those pesky wolves, for whom the forest was sanctuary. It wasn't until the 18th century that the deforestation trend was reversed, largely thanks to the aristocracy. The fourth Duke of Atholl, for example, planted 27.5 million trees between 1774 and 1830, and it is largely thanks to him and his dynasty that the drive up to Rannoch from Pitlochry is such a visual treat, particularly in autumn, when the mix of (mainly non-native) deciduous and evergreen trees – beech, birch, lime, larch, spruce, douglas fir – puts on a pyrotechnical display of tartan colours.

But as you drive steadily westwards, this woodland begins a slow striptease; in height, in species, in quantity, in density, it all begins to shrink away, until you reach the shores of Loch Rannoch itself, the front line in the war between wilderness and diversity. Apart from a couple of plantations of commercially grown sitka spruce, the trees here – ash, oak, hazel, birch and Caledonian pine – are half the size of their more exotic planted cousins to the east, but they are the tenacious natives in their original setting, and worthy of respect.

The main human settlement today is at Kinloch Rannoch, on the eastern end of the loch. It's a stolid Victorian village with a garage, a post office, and a couple of shops, and its main square is dominated by the Dunalastair, a creaky, traditional hotel, which is a popular base for hunting and shooting, with a log-fired drawing room ideal for afternoon tea and a dining room with stuffed salmon on the walls and antlers for chandeliers.

As for Loch Rannoch, it is a moody beast, and in parts up to 500 feet deep. On still days, the likes of the Schiehallion mountain – the fairy hill of the Caledonians and Perthshire's Mount Fuji – have their reflection etched on its surface of polished steel, and the shore-surrounding birch trees give tantalising glimpses of small sandy beaches. On wilder days, the wind funnels down the glen and the water rages like caged mercury.

Above all, this is a place of originals, a place to witness nature as it has always been. The red squirrels, the eagles, and the ospreys. The goosanders, the mergansers and the black-throated divers. The ABC of the Gaelic alphabet, Ailm (elm), Beith (birch) and Cole (hazel). You are, however, unlikely to meet a wolf.

The remote village of Kinloch Rannoch, on the east end of the loch, has been home to several clans over the centuries, including the Menzies, MacDougalls, Camerons and Robertsons.

OTHER BEAUTY SPOTS

The dominant mountain rising above Loch Rannoch eastern end, Schiehallion (3,547 feet), is a popular and not-too-difficult climb, but only in the right weather conditions. There's no point in setting off on a walk if the peak is in cloud. The best route starts from a car park on the edge of woodland, on the mountain's eastern flank. The land belongs to the John Muir Trust, which has made a great effort to create an accessible path with steps and a dry walking surface. Only the last mile has some challenging sections, involving a long clamber across extensive rock fields, but the views are tremendous. Allow yourself four hours to get up and down.

For something more sedentary, stop off at Queen's View on the B8019 overlooking Loch Tummel. High up among broadleaf woodland, it's a stirring viewpoint, but the extra ingredient here is the Forestry Commission visitor centre, which has good displays on the local ecology, and the tea-room. The queen it is named after is Victoria, who was a regular visitor to the area, although the monarch once said: 'it was called after me, although I had not been there in 1844'. She also complained that the cup of tea she had there was not hot. Hopefully yours will be better.

WHERE TO STAY & EAT

The village of Kinloch Rannoch has a fine example of a community-run eating place in Post Taste (01882 632333). As the name suggests, it doubles as a post office and internet café. The daytime offering is limited to soup, baked potatoes and home baking, but it has a more extensive menu in the evening (venison, steak and so on) – booking required. Rannoch Station also has a perfunctory café on the platform, good for shelter and something hot. But the best place for coffee or afternoon tea is the Dunalastair Hotel (01882 632323, www.dunalastair.co.uk), with its luxurious, sofa-stuffed drawing room.

The Loch Tummel Inn at Strath Tummel (01882 634272, www.lochtummelinn.co.uk) is a small old coaching inn with a fine view of Rannoch's neighbouring loch. The inn is friendly, unfussy and good quality, and the rooms are (mercifully) free of any tartan carpets. At the time of writing, the menu is limited to bar food, but the restaurant upstairs should be sensational when it's licensed.

For finer things, the East Haugh Hotel (01796 473121, www.easthaugh.co.uk), just outside Pitlochry, avoids the chintzy tartanitis of that town. Part boutique hotel and baronial Scottish manor, it is immaculate, stylish and family run. Everything is done properly and with flair. Meals feature seafood from Scotland's west coast (lobster, dover sole, surf clams) and game shot by the chef (grouse, pheasant, venison).

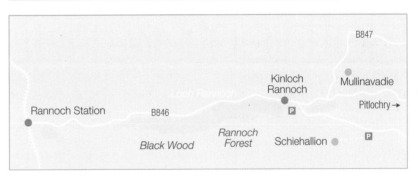

HOW TO GET THERE

Loch Rannoch is about 18 miles east of Pitlochry in Perthshire. **By road** The road to Loch Rannoch, the B847, branches off the main A9 just north of Pitlochry at Calvine. **By rail** The station at Pitlochry is served by trains from Glasgow and Edinburgh, while the station at Rannoch is served only from Glasgow. Both have overnight sleepers from London (08457 484950, www.scotrail.co.uk). **On foot** There is no footpath on the shore of Loch Rannoch, but you can walk the road. You can climb Schiehallion on a path from the car park on the loch's east shore or walk through Black Wood, on the loch's south shore, from the path at Carie. See also Walking Scotland (http://walking.visit scotland.com). **Map** Ordnance Survey Explorer 385, Rannoch Moor & Ben Alder; grid ref NN586578.

FURTHER REFERENCE

Pitlochry Tourist Office (01796 472751, www.perthshire.co.uk). Tay Forest Park (01350 727284, www.forestry.gov.uk).

Rothiemurchus

Magical faraway trees.

From a period starting 10,000 years ago, the last hurrah of the Ice Age, to about 4,000 years ago, when the local climate started to get colder and wetter, Scotland's forests enjoyed a long, golden morning of growth. As much as 60 per cent of the country's land mass came to be covered by the Ancient Wood of Caledon, the western extent of a biome that stretched across northern Europe. Initially there was alder, birch and willow, later came Scots pine and other species; bands of Mesolithic hunter-gatherer ranged along the coast, river valleys and finally ventured inland. Under the canopy of trees, they would have found aurochs, deer and elk, and predators such as brown bear, lynx and the grey wolf.

Man's initial impact on the wildwood was limited, mainly owing to the low population and rudimentary tools. But when climate change started in about 2000 BC, and agriculture supplanted the nomadic lifestyle, the forest began to shrink. Fast forward to the present day, via millennia of technology and woodland exploitation, and a mere one per cent of the Ancient Wood of Caledon survives. There are pockets across Scotland, but one of the few places where it reaches truly grand proportions is in Rothiemurchus, a rugged forest in the Cairngorms National Park.

The landscape is one of the few in Britain that can compare to those found in North America, Scandinavia or Siberia. At Rothiemurchus, the forest stretches for miles, a vista of pine-covered valleys and foothills rising quickly towards the subarctic plateau of the high Cairngorms. The bears and wolves may be long gone, but walk in the woodland – quietly, in the very early morning – and you could startle a solitary deer; herds roam the hillsides above. Crowd-pleasing red squirrels are common, otters less so, and you have to be very lucky to spot a pine marten or wildcat. Deep in the forest, where there are no tracks and no people, endangered capercaillie are more likely to be heard than seen. They have a distinctive call of clicks and pops; the males resemble hefty black grouse and their name derives from a Gaelic phrase translating as 'horse of the woods'; there are fewer than 2,000 left in the entire country. In the skies, however, you can spot resident raptors such as the golden eagle or osprey (in the summer), along with 170 other bird species.

Rothiemurchus is actually a privately owned estate, although managed in sympathetic style both for wildlife and visitors, and has been in the hands of the Grant family since the 16th century – a remarkable run of aristocratic stewardship. Make enquiries at the visitor centre, asking about the owner's title, and there are no airs and graces. Staff reply: 'He's Lord Huntingtower, but we all call him Johnnie.' His ancestor, Elizabeth Grant, was the author of *The Memoirs of a Highland Lady*. The book includes reminiscences of her years in Rothiemurchus in the early 19th century, providing insight into aristocratic Highland life before Queen Victoria's regular jaunts to Balmoral made it fashionable.

Two hundred years after Elizabeth was a regular, the estate is now a playground for the people (activities range from archery to white-water rafting), but its raison d'être is still the 25,000 acres of extraordinary countryside. The impossibly beautiful Loch an Eilein is a bite-sized morning stroll, while a climb up Scotland's third-highest mountain, Braeriach, is a more daunting undertaking. There are no seascapes here, or dramatic fjords, but this is the high land, Scotland's ceiling. Britain's tallest peak (Ben Nevis) may be on the west coast, but the rest of the top five are in the Cairngorms, all at 4,000 feet or more, rising from the plateau. As you walk among them, the inhuman scale of the surroundings makes

Rothiemurchus, seen from above with Loch an Eilein, is one of the last remnants of the Ancient Wood of Caledon, and a refuge for the red squirrel.

you feel like a speck on the planet's surface. This is the land of Ice Ages, extreme winter weather and steep glaciated valleys. The sense of solitude can be welcome, or frightening, particularly at the hill pass of Lairig Ghru. In this severe cleft in the mountains, between the Spey and the Dee rivers, only the crunch of your boots on the narrow track confirms that you exist. It's no surprise that nearby Ben Macdui is haunted by Am Fear Liath Mòr, the Big Grey Man, a spectre that can induce fear without even being seen.

Back in the Rothiemurchus woods, the atmosphere is more benign and less alien. You can gaze at the mountains rather than try to conquer them, and your senses are preoccupied with the aesthetics of nature. If the sun shines, the Scots pines are dark green, vibrant, with rust-bright bark, while waves of heather-covered ground fade to a distant tree line, a vista of brown and purple braes and blue skies. Touch the bark of an ancient tree and listen to the cawing of a carrion crow. But there is one sensation that is more intense than the others: the smell of the wild wood. It rises from the ground, from the pines, from 10,000 renewed seasons of life since the last glaciers melted away – a democratic sensation, exactly the same for the landowner and the passer-by. Given how much of Scotland was covered by the Ancient Wood of Caledon when our Mesolithic ancestors first ventured here, you could even say it smelled of home.

OTHER BEAUTY SPOTS

The remnants of the Ancient Wood of Caledon continue into Abernethy and Glenmore Forest in one vast sweep. Glenmore Forest, the eastern stretch, has Loch Morlich, a popular watersports centre with a beach. Glenmore Lodge, a mile east, is Scotland's national training centre for outdoors activities. All around here, trails and mountain bike tracks are infused with the sights and smells of Scots pine. Glenmore is also home to Britain's only herd of reindeer (there are daily tours to see the animals; phone 01479 861228). From Glenmore Lodge, a path heads north over the moorland to Abernethy Forest. The forest's main claim to fame is Loch Garten, a haven for ospreys. In 1916, the birds became extinct in Britain, but in 1954 a pair of Scandinavian osprey spent the summer here, and soon attracted others: there are now an estimated 148 pairs in Britain, mostly in Scotland. The Royal Society for the Protection of Birds has a visitor centre at Loch Garten (01479 831476, www.rspb.org.uk).

Finally, if you tire of the splendid forests, there are always those imposing hills with birds-eye plateaus. After a punishing climb, there is an unmatched grandeur in looking down on Loch Avon or Loch Eanaich. The funicular railway at Cairngorm itself (01479 861261, www.cairngormmountain.co.uk) takes you high for no effort whatsoever. But since you haven't earned the view, no wandering around is allowed. Some people say this is prudent environmental management – or it might just be Scotland's Presbyterian soul.

WHERE TO STAY & EAT

Aviemore is a tourist town with chains including a Hilton (01479 810661, www.hilton.co.uk) and the Aviemore Highland Resort (0844 879 9152, www.macdonaldhotels.co.uk). The Cairngorm Hotel (01479 810233, www.cairngorm.com) is more of a traditional lodge. Its

functional rooms won't win prizes for edgy decor, but it's got local character: there may be a Scottish accordionist in the bar, and mince and tatties in the restaurant.

Corrour House (01479 810220, www.corrourhousehotel.co.uk), in nearby Inverdruie, is a polite, Victorian establishment, originally built as a dower house for the Grants of Rothiemurchus, and still decorated with a whiff of period chintz. Further afield is the bucolic Cross at Kingussie (01540 661166, www.thecross.co.uk), a restaurant with rooms in an old tweed mill by the river; the civilised Boat Hotel at Boat of Garten (01479 831258, www.boathotel.co.uk), with traditional decor and a gourmet Scottish restaurant; and the homely Fairwinds at Carrbridge, a country retreat with a conservatory restaurant and seven acres with views of the Cairngorms (01479 841240, www.fairwindshotel.com).

In Aviemore, the Mountain Café (01479 812473, www.mountaincafe-aviemore.co.uk) does great breakfasts, cakes, soups, sandwiches and salads. Ord Bàn at the Rothiemurchus Centre (01479 810005, www.ordban.com) is a good café-restaurant that serves locally sourced bistro-style dishes. Finally, the Old Bridge Inn at Aviemore (01479 811137, www.oldbridgeinn.co.uk) serves pub grub and beer by a crackling fire.

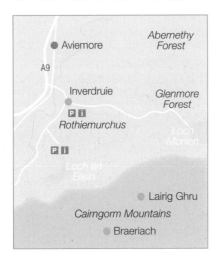

HOW TO GET THERE

Rothiemurchus is in the Cairngorms National Park in the Scottish Highlands. It is close to the hamlet of Inverdruie, but you can walk into the forest from Aviemore. **By road** Aviemore is on the main A9 road to Inverness, about 130 miles north of Edinburgh. **By train** Aviemore has a station on the line to Inverness. There are regular trains throughout the day from both Edinburgh and Glasgow (0845 601 5929, www.scotrail.co.uk). **By bus** The main bus services to Inverness pass through Aviemore: there are around five or six a day from Edinburgh and Glasgow (0870 550 5050, www.citylink.co.uk). **On foot** There are footpaths around Loch an Eilein by the car park and information centre, and paths throughout the forest. For maps, visit Rothiemurchus Visitor Centre. Bring stout shoes or boots, waterproof clothing and be prepared for severely cold weather in winter. Mountaineering courses are offered at Glenmore Lodge (01479 861256, www.glenmorelodge. org.uk). See also Walking Scotland (http://walking.visitscotland.com). **Map** Ordnance Survey Explorer 403, Cairn Gorm & Aviemore; grid ref NH936078.

FURTHER REFERENCE

Loch an Eilein Visitor Centre (01479 811085). Rothiemurchus Visitor Centre (01479 812345). For both, see www.rothiemurchus.net.

Loch Morlich lies in Glenmore Forest, home to Britain's only herd of reindeer.

Glen Affric

Beauty and the beasts.

The enduring cliché about Glen Affric is that it's the most beautiful glen in Scotland. For once, the merchants of hyperbole may be on to something. It benefits from obscurity, of course. Where the bonny banks of Loch Lomond are a short hop from Glasgow, and the imposing drama of Glencoe is something you pass through en route to Fort William, Glen Affric is a more distant and unfamiliar terminus. Hidden away in the wilderness west of Loch Ness, it sits behind the village of Cannich, remote and self-sufficient, sprinkled with lochs and enclosed by high mountains.

The rising lines of its horizon and the meandering loch shores create an aesthetic that almost bypasses conscious appreciation and seeps into your soul. The trees only enhance this sensation. Glen Affric is home to remnants of the Ancient Wood of Caledon, the wildwood that flourished after the last Ice Age. On a fine autumn day, the colours are magnificent: orange-gold, brown and intense green. More than just a pretty picture, however, this pine forest is a biological thread to another epoch, connecting the present to a time when the glaciers were retreating, and linking us with our forebears, as well as the beasts of long ago and the wildlife of today: 10,000 years in one place.

A little way into the glen at Coire Loch, for example, you can find more than a dozen species of dragonfly in season, hovering like bit players from a boreal myth. Glen Affric is also home to pine marten, golden eagle, osprey, red deer, roe deer, capercaillie and otter. Nobody knows for sure when the brown bear population was wiped out – perhaps during the time of the Roman occupation of Britain. The wolf probably persisted until the 17th century; this is just the kind of far-flung tract where the animal could have clung on to a dwindling, marginal existence.

Looking around the glen, even in summer sunshine, you could still imagine packs of grey wolves here. The dense forest in the east would certainly provide cover. And when the weather turns foul – and it will in the Scottish Highlands – the glen is truly wild at heart.

Indeed, some swear that Glen Affric comes into its own when you can almost touch the clouds and the light is weak, as perverse as that may seem. But be warned: in bleak conditions, it's the slouching beasts of the mind, rather than the predatory creatures of record, that cause anxiety. Driving the road from Cannich on a wet afternoon, when the trees look black and there are no other cars, those of nervous disposition might feel they've chanced upon a menacing film location. Indeed, *Dog Soldiers*, a 2002 British horror movie involving a doomed army patrol and werewolves, was filmed here, as was *Wilderness*, a 1990s TV series about a librarian-turned werewolf. It's no wonder that a party of tourists once reportedly fled Glen Affric, thinking they heard a werewolf howl. This tale may sound far-fetched, but if you're here, feeling the low pressure of a clinging, meteorological depression, it is easy to imagine something supernatural beyond the next bend.

Go to Loch Affric, near the end of the Glen, and the spooky atmosphere intensifies. If rain is pelting in from the west, there won't be anyone else around as the low hills play peek-a-boo through the gloom. The real mountains are invisible, 3,000 feet high, biding their time in the cloudbanks, forming a firewall around the sparse west end of the glen. As you walk, there is a sense of encroachment, enclosure and that enduring unease. Beyond Loch Affric, the eco-hostel at Alltbeithe is an old stalking bothy in the navel of nowhere (it is eight miles from the nearest road and there are no signs).

This is rugged country. On the track above the north shore of Loch Affric, you have to cross the torrents coming off the hills and negotiate slick rocks with all the grace of a drunk. Soak up the scene of slate black water, pine silhouettes and dense wildwood, hills angled off into nothing and the subtle chaos of that changing grey sky. It's more complex than the picture-postcard scenery with which Glen Affric is normally associated. In the rain, Glen Affric is an education in natural history, but one that is acquired through the senses: you can almost feel those bears and wolves out there in the mist.

By contrast, when the sun shines, when the light sparkles from the lochs and the river, when there's a dusting of snow on the high tops or heather colouring the braes, a deer glimpsed in the distance, more dragonflies than you can count and a golden eagle on the wing for good measure, then this is merely the most beautiful glen in Scotland.

OTHER BEAUTY SPOTS

There is something exhilarating about landscapes of wild Highland rivers and large bodies of water enclosed by mountains – vistas that are commonplace around Cannich and Glen Affric. At Glen Cannich, you can embark on an eight-mile meander through the hills to Loch Mullardoch. Though dammed not long after World War II for a hydro scheme. it's still both remote and stunning, and its shores provide access to some hefty mountains on the north side. (To get to Glen Cannich, take the minor road north-west from Cannich.)

Glen Urquhart, east of Cannich, is not nearly as sparse or unpopulated as Glen Cannich (and you don't have to drive along a single-track road). It leads to Urquhart Bay on Loch Ness, and the iconic Urquhart Castle, a ruin that has stood here since the Dark

When the sun is shining, this is the most beautiful glen in Scotland, but the solitude can also be scary; Affric Lodge (next page).

Ages. Sit a while and look for the monster (the greatest number of Nessie sightings have occurred here). Or just dwell on the idea of the Great Glen, a massive geological fault that runs from Inverness to Fort William through lochs Ness, Oich, Lochy and Linnhe.

Strathfarrar, north-east of Cannich, is a landscape of forest and loch, waterfalls and hills. If you follow the valley west for 15 miles, you'll come to the pristine Loch Monar, with imposing peaks all around. The minor road up Strathfarrar is private, however; it's usually open to cyclists and walkers, but check with the tourist office at Inverness (*see p239*) for details of vehicle access.

WHERE TO STAY & EAT

The Tomich Hotel (01456 415399, www.tomichhotel.co.uk), near Cannich, is a Victorian hunting lodge with a cosy feel (log fires throughout) and helpful staff who will direct you to nearby sights (such as the lovely Plodda Falls). The traditional restaurant serves Scottish cuisine (at breakfast, you can have haggis, tattie scones and black pudding). And the place oozes history: Churchill and Gladstone both stayed here and the golden retriever was first bred on this estate in the 1860s.

Polmaily Country Hotel (01456 450343, www.polmaily.co.uk), east of the Glen towards Loch Ness, is a small, family-oriented country house, with pleasant gardens and

The birch trees around Loch Beinn A Mheadhoin are at their flaming best during the autumn.

a swimming pool. In nearby Lewiston, the Loch Ness Inn (01456 450991, www.staylochness.co.uk) is an old brewery done up with a modern, functional interior. The restaurant could rustle up some Applecross prawns to start, or venison sausages as a main. The nearby village of Drumnadrochit has a range of B&Bs. The best is the 19th-century Rowan Cottage (01456 450944, www.rowancottagebedandbreakfast.co.uk), which is tiny and popular (open April to November). North of Loch Ness, the Lovat Arms (01463 782313, www.lovatarms.com) is a traditional but stylish Highland hotel in the village of Beauly, with a brasserie that serves beef, game and fish from local estates.

In Inverness, tourist capital of the Highlands and 26 miles from Glen Affric, the rooms at the Glenmoriston Townhouse Hotel (01463 223777, www.glenmoristontownhouse.com) have metropolitan chic, while its Abstract restaurant offers up-to-the-minute Franco-Scots cooking. In 2009, the Roux brothers came to Inverness, opening the edgy Rocpool hotel (01463 240089, www.rocpool.com); Chez Roux, its restaurant, is fashionable and French.

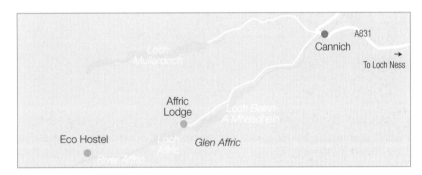

HOW TO GET THERE

Glen Affric is in the Scottish Highlands 26 miles south-west of Inverness. **By road** From Inverness, a car is the easiest option. Either head south down Loch Ness on the A82 then turn west at Drumnadrochit, following the A831 to Cannich, or go west of Inverness on the A862, turning off on to the A831 and following this road into Strathglass and down to Cannich. From Cannich, follow the minor road south-west past Dog Falls to Loch Beinn 'Mheadhoin, and beyond to Loch Affric. **By air** Inverness is the nearest airport. **By train** Inverness is the nearest station (National Rail Enquiries, 08457 484950). **By bus** There are buses from Inverness to Cannich, around three a day (Traveline, 0871 200 2233). **On foot** The walk around Loch Affric from the car park at the loch's east end is ten miles. For shorter walks, the car park for Dog Falls (between Fasnakyle Forest and Loch Beinn a' Mheadhoin) has boards with details of shorter tracks that go to the falls, Coire Loch and to a viewpoint over the glen. See also Walking Scotland (http://walking.visitscotland.com). **Map** Ordnance Survey Explorer 415, Glen Affric & Glen Moriston; grid ref H156222.

FURTHER REFERENCE

There is a tourist information centre in Inverness on Castle Wynd (08452 255121, www.visitscotland.com). See also http://walking.visitscotland.com.

Inverpolly

Out of this world.

Inverpolly may be part of the Scottish Highlands, but its scenery is less *Monarch of the Glen* than something from science fiction. Whereas much of the Highlands are covered with bonny postcard scenery and pine forests – as in Rothiemurchus – Inverpolly is positively alien; and whereas large stretches of Scotland tend to rise gradually to a high plateau – like the Cairngorms – at Inverpolly, the freakish mountains pop up out of nowhere. Forgotten in Scotland's empty north-west corner, between the Assynt mountains and the open Atlantic, Inverpolly is a landscape that is strange and sublime, barren yet beautiful. Trees are conspicuous by their absence, peat bog stretches for miles, the moorland is scarred with rock that appears to belong on another planet, and there are more lochs and lochans here than most people would deem reasonable, or indeed terrestrial. Roads are absent, vast areas only accessible on foot, and man-made structures are few – this is one of the least-populated corners of Europe. To top it off, the clouds that roll in off the Atlantic create otherworldly tricks of light.

If photographers are in their element here, so are geologists. Major fault lines divide Scotland into distinct regions, and the North West Highlands (considered anything north-west of the Great Glen between Inverness and Fort William), are a law unto themselves. But the coastal strip near Inverpolly is even more distinctive: it is separated from the rest of the North West Highlands by the Moine Thrust of mountains, formed 400 million years ago when Scandinavia crashed into Greenland (which was then attached to Scotland). Along this long sliver of land, older rocks have been pushed above younger ones, thanks to tectonic rumblings; the oldest natural furniture around here, Lewisian Gneiss, dates back almost three billion years. The thrust phenomenon, along with erosion and glaciation, have created the most sparse and idiosyncratic landscape in Britain.

Take Stack Polly – or Stac Pollaidh if you speak Gaelic – a 2,000-foot, craggy pinnacle: its jagged ridge shares design values with the stegosaurus and Shane MacGowan's teeth before he got them fixed. The pin-up girl for Inverpolly is the stark Suilven, a vertiginous, 2,400-foot sugarloaf mountain whose striking shape has also been compared to a sphinx. Then there is Cul Mor (2,700 feet), whose twin peaks have a wild grandeur, and its sister Cul Beag (2,500 feet), another 'inselberg', a term used by geologists that means 'island mountains' – isolated peaks that rise abruptly.

Stack Polly may be an icon, but hikers say it is relatively easy to reach the ridge (scaling the peak is far riskier). A very obvious path has been carved out, and people even take their children up for a relatively straightforward Highland jaunt. Visually, it delivers a lot of bang per buck. From the ridge, you have an almost god-like perspective of this alien landscape, all peculiar peaks, pockmarked terrain and stunted fauna, set against the complicated shoreline of Loch Sionasgaig. The sheer number and pattern of lochs resemble an illustration in a book about chaos theory.

The panorama is magnificent, but it would likely baffle artists like Constable or Turner. Perhaps abstract expressionists would have better luck depicting this spongy, peaty answer to Colorado's eerie Monument Valley. Its Gaelic meaning is 'Peat Moss at the Confluence of Waters'; if you're caught in the rain, up to your knees in mire, Bogmouth seems more appropriate.

From Stack Polly, you can also see the Atlantic coast and its intricate patterns of inlets, bays and rivers, and the Summer Isles beyond. The latter are barely inhabited, except for seabirds and the sheep that are moved here for summer grazing (hence the name).

Inverpolly may not be an island, but it feels similarly detached from this world. It is a long way, in distance and in feel, from the bucolic charm of southern England. And it's all down to geology: the rocks underfoot are the wrong way round, old above new, and this unsettling inversion hangs in the air. This is strange, sublime Scotland – the final frontier.

OTHER BEAUTY SPOTS

In the open Atlantic, west of Inverpolly, lie the splendid Summer Isles. Though they inspired the name Summerisle, the setting for the 1973 film *The Wicker Man*, they are virtually uninhabited, so the chances of finding pagan rituals, or Britt Ekland dancing, are slim. But you will see seals and sea birds, and maybe porpoises and Minke whales, if you take a boat trip there (either from Ullapool or Achiltibuie, *see p247*).

For more Inverpolly-style drama, explore the North West Highlands Geopark – vast mountainous terrain bordered by the Summer Isles in the south and west, the north coast of Sutherland, and the Moine Thrust in the east. So empty is the region that even the visitor centre at Knockan Crag is not staffed, but there are good displays and scenic walks.

For a lake, mountain and sea spectacular, do the 'Lochinver loop'. From Ullapool, drive to Loch Assynt (take the A835 and A837), follow its shoreline west, then veer on to the B869 at Lochinver, a whitewashed fishing village. This coastal road passes splendid little beaches at Clachtoll and Clashnessie, a photogenic viewpoint at Drumbeg, and the startling mountain of Quinag. At Kylesku, you can take a boat trip up Loch Glencoul and gaze at the highest waterfall in Britain (658 feet, at Eas a Chual Aluinn).

The views from the top of Stack Polly are spectacular (previous page), and its jagged ridge also looks striking from below (left). The River Garvie (next page) flows from nearby Loch Osgaig into the sea.

For more soul food, marvel at the mountains and sea on the minor road between Lochinver and Achiltibuie, a cliff-top village overlooking the Summer Isles.

Inverewe Garden, west of Ullapool, is a significant trek from Inverpolly (about a two-hour drive), but it is a botanical wonder. Thanks to the Gulf Stream, the climate here is mild and the foliage lush, with palm trees and exotic plants from around the globe.

WHERE TO STAY & EAT

The Summer Isles Hotel at Achiltibuie (01854 622282, www.summerisleshotel.co.uk) is a local legend. Its white cottages overlook the eponymous islands; the decor is crisp and chic; and the restaurant has earned a Michelin star (a five-course dinner might include scallop mousse, wood pigeon and Lochinver halibut). Its bar, open to non-residents, serves superior sandwiches and cask ale. (Note: the hotel is closed from November to March.)

Albannach at Lochinver (01571 844407, www.thealbannach.co.uk) also has stylish bedrooms and a Michelin-starred restaurant, where a five-course meal could include local crab tartlet, butternut squash soup, roast venison and hot chocolate soufflé.

Otherwise in Lochinver, the Caberfeidh (01571 844321, www.thecaberfeidh.co.uk) does pub grub, while the Lochinver Larder Riverside Bistro (01571 844356) operates as a café, shop and bistro; the same people make renowned pies (www.piesbypost.co.uk).

South of Lochinver, by the hamlet of Inverkirkaig, Achins Bookshop and Coffee Shop (01571 844262, www.scotbooks.freeuk.com) is a startlingly unexpected café-bookshop. Meanwhile, the Inchnadamph Hotel, on the A837 near Loch Assynt (01571 822202, www.inchnadamphhotel.co.uk) is a basic hostelry, popular with anglers and walkers.

Cul Beag, viewed from the shores of Loch Lurgainn, is an 'inselberg' – a mountain that rises abruptly from a plain, like so many peaks in and around Inverpolly.

Nearby Ullapool is full of options. The Ceilidh Place (01854 612103, www. theceilidhplace.com), a huge cottage, has culture and character. The simple bedrooms are filled with books. There's also a bunkhouse, café-bar, library and a bookshop. For meals, you might have lamb and heather ale casserole or venison braised with red wine.

HOW TO GET THERE

Inverpolly is in the far north-west of Scotland, between Ullapool and Lochinver; the landscape described here also takes in Assynt (to the north) and Coigach (to the south). **By road** About 10 miles north of Ullapool on the A835, a minor road on the left leads to Inverpolly. This road passes the car park under Stack Polly. Alternatively, from Lochinver, there is a minor road heading south into Inverpolly via Inverkirkaig. **By train** Inverness is the nearest station, but it is 70 miles away (National Rail Enquiries, 08457 484950). **By bus** There is a very limited local bus service around Inverpolly (0871 200 2233, www.traveline.org.uk). **By air** Inverness has the nearest airport (01667 462445, www.hial.co.uk). **By boat** To see the Summer Isles, in season, take the Summer Queen from Ullapool (01854 612472, www.summerqueen. co.uk) or Summer Isles Cruises from Achiltibuie (01854 622200, www. summer-isles-cruises.co.uk). For boat trips from Kylesku to see the waterfall, contact the Kylesku Hotel (01971 502231, www.kyleskuhotel.co.uk). **On foot** To ascend Stack Polly, take the path from the car park on the minor road by Loch Lurgainn, five miles west of the A835. The circular two-mile path climbs about 1,600 feet. It can be steep but it's not too hard to reach the ridge; trying to reach the true summit along the top is dangerous. There are several paths at Inverpolly: east of Stack Polly car park, one by Loch Lurgainn starts at a roadside cairn, near a wood of Scots pines. See also http://walking.visitscotland.com. **Map** Ordnance Survey Explorer 439/442; Colgach & Summer Isles/Assynt & Lochinver; grid ref NC115118.

FURTHER REFERENCE

There are seasonal tourist information centres at Ullapool and Lochinver (for both, 08452 255121, www.visitscotland. com). Inverewe Garden (01445 781200, www.nts.org.uk). Knockan Crag Nature Reserve (01854 613418, www.knockan-crag.co.uk). North-West Highlands Geopark (01571 844000, www.north west-highlands-geopark.org.uk).

Further reference

For additional websites relating to a specific area, see the information box at the end of each chapter.

BEACHES/COAST
Adopt a Beach, www.adoptabeach.org.uk
BBC Coast, www.bbc.co.uk/coast
Beachcombing, www.glaucus.org.uk/hightide.htm
Blue Flag Beaches, www.blueflag.org
Cornwall Beach Guide, www.cornwall-beaches.co.uk
Good Beach Guide, www.goodbeachguide.co.uk
Marine Conservation Society, www.mcsuk.org
Seawatch Foundation,
    www.seawatchfoundation.org.uk
UK Marine Special Areas of Conservation,
    www.ukmarinesac.org.uk
UNESCO Dorset and East Devon Coast,
    www.jurassiccoast.com

BUS
First Group, www.firstgroup.com
National Express, www.nationalexpress.co.uk
Traveline, 0871 200 2233, www.traveline.org.uk

CAMPING
Camping & Caravanning Club,
    www.campingandcaravanningclub.co.uk
Camping, Caravan & Touring Holiday Directory,
    www.campinguk.com
Scottish Camping & Caravanning,
    www.scottishcamping.com
UK Caravan & Campsite Directory,
    www.ukcampsite.co.uk/sites

CYCLING
Byways & Bridleways Trust, www.bbtrust.org.uk
British Cycling, www.britishcycling.org.uk
Cycling Wales, www.cycling.visitwales.co.uk
Cycling Scotland, http://cycling.visitscotland.com
International Mountain Biking Association UK,
    www.imba.org.uk
National Cycle Network, www.ctc.org.uk
Tandem Club, www.tandem-club.org.uk
Trail Cyclist Association, www.trailquest.co.uk
Sustrans, www.sustrans.org.uk

DISABLED
Bike for All, www.bikeforall.net
DisAbility Holidays.net, www.disabilityholidays.net
Holiday Care Services, www.holidaycare.org.uk
Tourism for All, www.tourismforall.org.uk
Wheelchair Travel & Access Minibuses,
    www.wheelchair-travel.co.uk
Wheels for All, http://cpnw.newcomweb.demon.com

ENVIRONMENTAL & CONSERVATION ORGANISATIONS
Association for the Protection of Rural Scotland,
    www.ruralscotland.org
British Association of Nature Conservationists,
    www.banc.org.uk

British Marine Life Study Centre,
    www.glaucus.org.uk
Campaign for the Protection of Rural England,
    www.cpre.org.uk
Campaign for the Protection of Rural Wales,
    www.cprw.org.uk
Carbon Footprint, www.carbonfootprint.com
Environment Agency,
    www.environment-agency.gov.uk
Environmental Protection UK, www.nsca.org.uk
Forestry Commision, www.forestry.gov.uk
Friends of the Earth, www.foe.co.uk
Greenpeace, www.greenpeace.org.uk
**Marine Life Information Network for Britain
    and Ireland**, www.marlin.ac.uk
Moorland Association,
    www.moorlandassociation.org
Natural England, www.naturalengland.org.uk
Tree Register, www.treeregister.org
The Woodland Trust, www.british-trees.com
World Wide Fund for Nature, www.wwf.org.uk

FISHING
Environment Agency Fishing Regulations,
    www.environment-agency.gov.uk/subjects/fish
Fishing in Scotland, www.fishpal.com/visitscotland
Fishing Wales, www.fishing.visitwales.com

GEOLOGY
British Geological Survey, www.bgs.ac.uk
UK Fossil Collecting Locations, www.ukfossils.co.uk

HERITAGE ORGANISATIONS
Cadw (the official guardian of the built heritage of
    Wales), www.cadw.wales.gov.uk
English Heritage, www.english-heritage.org.uk
International Council on Monuments & Sites UK,
    www.icomos-uk.org
Landmark Trust, www.landmarktrust.org.uk
National Trust, www.nationaltrust.org.uk
National Trust for Scotland, www.nts.org.uk
Scottish National Heritage, www.snh.org.uk
UK World Heritage Sites,
    www.culture.gov.uk/ukwhportal
UNESCO, www.unesco.org

HORSE RIDING
British Horse Society, www.bhs.org.uk
Byways & Bridleways Trust, www.bbtrust.org.uk

MAPS
Ordnance Survey, www.ordnancesurvey.co.uk

MYSTIC BRITAIN
Stone-Circles.Org.Uk, www.stone-circles.org.uk
Mysterious Britain & Ireland,
    www.mysteriousbritain.co.uk

NATURISM

Bare Britain, www.barebritain.com
British Naturism, www.british-naturism.org.uk/beaches
Naturist UK Fact File, http://nuff.org.uk

PUBS

Good Pub Guide, www.thegoodpubguide.co.uk

SAFETY

British Activity Holiday Association or Safe Quality Activity Holidays, www.baha.org.uk
Cairngorm Mountain Rescue Team, www.cmrt.org.uk
Mountain Rescue England & Wales, www.mountain.rescue.org.uk
Royal National Lifeboat Institution (RNLI), www.rnli.org.uk
Royal Life Saving Society UK, www.lifesavers.org.uk

SPORTS

British Association of Balloon Operators www.babo.org.uk
British Canoe Union, www.bcu.org.uk
British Hang Gliding and Paragliding Association, www.bhpa.co.uk
British Waterski Online, www.britishwaterski.org.uk
British Sub Aqua Club, www.bsac.com
British Sub Aqua Club Snorkelling, www.bsacsnorkelling.co.uk
England's Golf Coast, www.englandsgolfcoast.com
Fell Runners Association, www.fellrunner.org.uk
Geocaching, (worldwide GPS based treasure hunt) www.geocaching.com
Golf Scotland www.golfscotland.com
Go-Paddle www.go-paddle.co.uk
The Kite Society of Great Britain www.thekitesociety.org.uk
Royal Yachting Association, www.rya.org.uk
Sussex Hang Gliding and Paragliding, www.sussexhgpg.co.uk
UKClimbing.com, www.ukclimbing.com
UK Windsurfing Association, www.ukwindsurfing.com

SWIMMING

Lidos in the UK (including tidal saltwater pools), www.lidos.org.uk
Swim Trek Adventure Holidays, www.swimtrek.com
Wild Swimming, www.wildswimming.co.uk

SURFING

A1 Surf, www.a1surf.com
British Surfing Association, www.britsurf.co.uk

TOURISM

EnjoyEngland, www.enjoyengland.com
Undiscovered Scotland, www.undiscoveredscotland.co.uk
Visit Britain, www.visitbritain.com
Visit Scotland, www.visitscotland.com
Visit Wales, www.visitwales.com

TRAIN INFORMATION

Heart of Wales Railway, www.heart-of-wales.co.uk
National Rail Enquiries, 0871 200 4950, www.nationalrail.co.uk
North Yorkshire Moors Railway, www.nymr.co.uk
Settle-Carlisle Railway, www.settle-carlisle.co.uk
Train Line, www.thetrainline.com

TRANSPORT PLANNING

AA Route Planner, www.theaa.com/travelwatch
BBC Travel News, www.bbc.co.uk/travelnews
Traveline, 0871 200 2233, www.traveline.org.uk

WALKING

British Orienteering, www.britishorienteering.org.uk
Countryside Access, (including the Countryside Code) www.countrysideaccess.gov.uk
Go4awalk.com, www.go4awalk.com
Hillwalking, www.hillwalking.org.uk
Long Distance Walkers Association, www.ldwa.org.uk
National Trail, (including the Ridgeway, Thames Path, Cleveland Way & Penine Way), www.nationaltrail.co.uk
Ramblers Association, www.ramblers.org.uk
Scottish Orienteering, www.scottish-orienteering.org
South West Coastal Path, www.southwestcoastpath.com
The Wainwright Society, www.wainwright.org.uk
Walking Englishman, www.walkingenglishman.com
Walklink.com, www.walklink.com
Walking-Routes, www.walking-routes.co.uk

WEATHER

Met Office, www.metoffice.gov.uk
BBC Weather, http://news.bbc.co.uk/weather

WILDLIFE

Badger Trust, www.badger.org.uk
Bat Conservation Trust, www.bats.org.uk
Botanical Society of the British Isles, www.bsbi.org.uk
British Dragonfly Society, www.dragonflysoc.org.uk
British Trust for Ornithology, www.bto.org.uk
Butterfly Conservation, www.butterfly-conservation.org
Dolphin Care, www.dolphincareuk.org
Mammal Society, www.mammal.org.uk
RSPB, www.rspb.org.uk
RSPCA, www.rspca.org.uk
Seabird Group, www.seabirdgroup.org.uk
Sea Bird Colonies Scotland, www.ntsseabirds.org.uk
Save Our Seals, www.saveourseals.co.uk
Scotland's National Nature Reserves, www.nnr-scotland.org.uk
Scottish Wildlife Trust, www.swt.org.uk
Seal Sanctuary UK, www.sealsanctuary.co.uk
Shark Trust UK, www.sharktrust.org
Whale & Dolphin Conservation Society, www.wdcs.org.uk
Wild About Britain, www.wildaboutbritain.co.uk
Wildfowl and Wetland Trust, www.wwt.org.uk
Wildlife Trusts, www.wildlifetrusts.org

YOUTH HOSTELS

Scottish Youth Hostels Association, www.syha.org.uk
UK Youth Hostels Association, www.yha.org.uk

Where to go for…